CW00553412

American Colonial Ranger

Ranger

The Northern Colonies 1724–64

Gary Zaboly

First published in Great Britain in 2004 by Osprey Publishing, Elms Court, Chapel Way, Botley,
Oxford OX2 9LP, United Kingdom.
Email: info@ospreypublishing.com

© 2004 Osprey Publishing Ltd.

All rights reserved. Apart from any fair dealing for the purpose of private study, research, criticism or review, as permitted under the Copyright, Designs and Patents Act, 1988, no part of this publication may be reproduced, stored in a retrieval system, or transmitted in any form or by any means, electronic, electrical, chemical, mechanical, optical, photocopying, recording or otherwise, without the prior written permission of the copyright owner. Enquiries should be addressed to the Publishers.

A CIP catalog record for this book is available from the British Library.

ISBN 1 84176 649 6

Gary Zaboly has asserted his right under the Copyright, Designs and Patents Act, 1988, to be identified as the Author and Illustrator of this Work.

Editor: Gerard Barker
Design: Ken Vail Graphic Design, Cambridge, UK
Index by Glyn Sutcliffe
Originated by Grasmere Digital Imaging, Leeds, UK
Printed in China through World Print Ltd.

04 05 06 07 08   10 9 8 7 6 5 4 3 2 1

FOR A CATALOG OF ALL BOOKS PUBLISHED BY OSPREY MILITARY AND AVIATION PLEASE CONTACT:

Osprey Direct USA, c/o MBI Publishing, P.O. Box 1, 729 Prospect Ave, Osceola, WI 54020, USA
E-mail: info@ospreydirectusa.com

Osprey Direct UK, P.O. Box 140, Wellingborough, Northants, NN8 2FA, UK
E-mail: info@ospreydirect.co.uk

www.ospreypublishing.com

Artist's note

Readers may care to note that the original paintings from which the color plates in this book were prepared are available for private sale. All reproduction copyright whatsoever is retained by the Publishers. All enquiries should be addressed to:

Gary Zaboly
500 Kappock Street Apt 6F
Riverdale
Bronx
NY
10463-6410
U.S.A.

The Publishers regret that they can enter into no correspondence upon this matter.

CONTENTS

THE AMERICAN COLONIAL RANGER: THE NORTHERN COLONIES 1724–64

INTRODUCTION

Along the frontiers of the northern American colonies, where most of the battles of the French and Indian War took place, rangers proved indispensable adjuncts to the main regular and provincial armies, both as partisan warriors and as scouts. Backwoodsmen – hunters, trappers, militiamen, and Indian fighters – generally made the best rangers. But as tough and effective as the rangers often were, some British commanders were slow to give them credit. "The worst soldiers in the universe," James Wolfe called them. "It would be better they were all gone than have such a Riotous sort of people," complained Lieutenant-colonel William Haviland.

Yet the very qualities that these commanders despised in the rangers – their field attire that often resembled that of "savage" Indians, their unconventional tactics, their occasional obstreperousness, their democratic recruiting standards that allowed blacks and Indians into their ranks – are what helped make them uniquely adroit at fighting their formidable Canadian and Indian wilderness foes, in all kinds of weather conditions and environments.

Enlightened redcoat generals such as Brigadier George Augustus Howe, older brother of William, recognized that the forest war could not be won without rangers. Howe was so firmly convinced of this that in 1758 he persuaded Major-General James Abercromby to revamp his entire army into the image of the rangers, dress-wise, arms-wise, and drill-wise. Major-General Jeffrey Amherst, who would orchestrate the eventual conquest of Canada, championed Major Robert Rogers and his ranger corps as soon as he became the new commander-in-chief in late 1758. "I shall always cheerfully receive Your opinion in relation to the Service you are Engaged in," he promised Rogers. In the summer of 1759, Amherst's faith in the rangers was rewarded when, in the process of laying siege to Fort Carillon at Ticonderoga, they again proved themselves the only unit in the army sufficiently skilled to deal with the enemy's bushfighters. Even

Three rangers prepare to leave Rogers' Island on a winter scout in early 1758. Each man is equipped with ice creepers and snowshoes, and the ranger at right carries ice skates. (Author's drawing)

4

the general's vaunted Louisbourg light infantry received Amherst's wrath after two night attacks by Indians had resulted in 18 of their number killed and wounded, mostly from friendly fire.

Before the year was out, Rogers had burned the Abenaki village of Odanak, on the distant St Francis River, its warriors the long-time scourge of the New England frontier. In 1760, after the rangers had spearheaded the expulsion of French troops from the Richelieu River valley, Amherst sent Rogers and his men to carry the news of Montreal's surrender to the French outposts lying nearly 1,000 miles (1,600km) to the west. He sent them because they were the only soldiers in his 17,000-man army able to accomplish the task.

CHRONOLOGY

Battles with Native American warriors in the early 17th century had demonstrated the virtual uselessness of European armor, pikes, cavalry, and maneuvers in the dense New World forests. Although New England militia units had proven themselves courageous and adaptable during the horrific baptism of fire with local tribes known as King Philip's War, in 1676–77, it was not until the early 1700s that the colonists could produce frontiersmen capable of penetrating deep into uncharted Indian territory. In 1709, for instance, Captain Benjamin Wright took 14 rangers on a 400-mile (640km) round trip by canoe, up the Connecticut River, across the Green Mountains, and to the northern end of Lake Champlain, along the way fighting four skirmishes with Indians.

A 1756 map, "the Principal Seat of War." Robert Rogers was raised on the Merrimack valley frontier (the river's mouth can be seen just above Cape Ann). In company with John Stark and other future rangers he sometimes trapped as far north as the "White Hills," in the very heart of Abenaki hunting country. "Pigwacket Pond" is where Lovewell's rangers battled Paugus' Indians in 1725. (Author's collection)

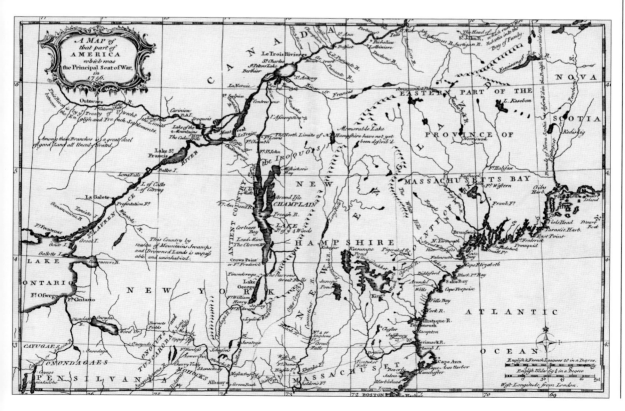

The garrison of Reverend Timothy Walker, in Concord, New Hampshire, as it probably looked during the French and Indian raids of the late 1740s. In a fort like this, young Robert Rogers and his family often found refuge after word of enemy incursions arrived at their farm, 10 miles (16km) to the south. (Author's collection)

The "Indian hunters" under Massachusetts' Captain John Lovewell were among the most effective of the early rangers. Their long, hard-fought battle at Lovewell's Pond on 9 May 1725, against Pigwacket Abenakis under the bearskin-robed war chief Paugus, became a watershed event in New England frontier history. Its story was told around hearths and campfires for decades, and its example informed future rangers that Indian warriors were not always invincible in the woods.

When the third war for control of North America broke out in 1744 (commonly called King George's War, after George II), several veterans of Lovewell's fight raised their own ranger companies and passed on their valuable field knowledge. Among the recruits who joined one company assigned to scout the upper Merrimack River valley around Rumford (later Concord), New Hampshire, was the teenager Robert Rogers.

Incessant French and Indian inroads turned the war of 1744–48 into a largely defensive one for the northern colonies. Log stockades and blockhouses protected refugee frontier families; Rumford itself had 12 such "garrison houses." When not on patrol or pursuing enemy raiders, rangers acted as armed guards for workers in the field. Bells and cannon from the forts sounded warnings when the enemy was detected in the vicinity.

At the beginning of the last French and Indian War, each newly raised provincial regiment generally included one or two ranger companies: men lightly dressed and equipped to serve as quick-reaction strike forces as well as scouts and intelligence gatherers. The near-annihilation of Braddock's army on the Monongahela, on 9 July 1755, made starkly evident the need to raise additional bodies of rangers. The Duke of Cumberland, Captain General of the British Army, not only encouraged their raising but also advised that some regular troops would have to reinvent themselves along ranger lines before wilderness campaigns could be won.

Nevertheless, it was not until after the shocking 1757 fall of Fort William Henry that plans were finally accelerated to counterbalance the large numbers of Canadian and Indian partisans. Captain Robert Rogers' ranger corps became the primary model for the eventual transformation of the regular and provincial army in that region. That the 1758 campaign against Ticonderoga failed, however, was not the fault of the radical modifications that were made, but rather of General Abercromby's hasty launching of a conventional frontal attack against Montcalm's formidable entrenchments. Elsewhere that year, particularly at Louisbourg and Fort Duquesne, similar uniform and accouterment renovations had also been made, but better leadership had provided victories.

Colonial irregulars aside from Rogers' men also contributed to the success of British arms during the war: provincial units such as Israel Putnam's Connecticut rangers, companies of Stockbridge Mahican and Connecticut Mohegan Indians, Joseph Gorham's and George Scott's Nova Scotia rangers, and home-based companies such as Captain Hezekiah Dunn's, on the New Jersey frontier. During Pontiac's War (1763–64), ranger companies led by such captains as Thomas Cresap and James Smith mustered to defend Maryland and Pennsylvania border towns and valleys.

RECRUITMENT AND ENLISTMENT

Rogers' rangers, the most famous, active, and influential colonial partisan body of the French and Indian War, never enjoyed the long-term establishment of a British regular regiment, with its permanent officer cadre, nor were they classed as a regiment or a battalion as the annually raised provincial troops were. In fact, at its peak Rogers' command was merely a collection, or corps, of short-term, independently raised ranger companies. Technically, "Rogers' rangers"

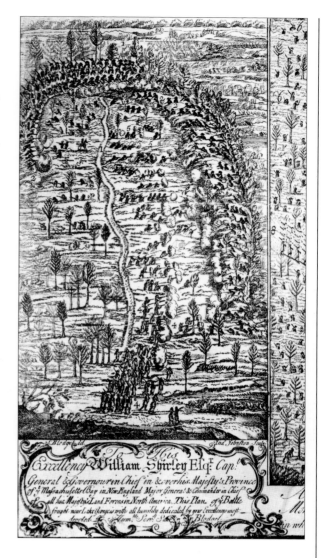

Detail from Samuel Blodgett's Perspective Plan of the Battle near Lake George, 1755, a rare contemporary depiction of a French and Indian ambush. The U-shaped trap was a favorite tactic of partisan warfare; Robert Rogers himself walked into one on at least two occasions. Blodgett was a soldier in Colonel Blanchard's New Hampshire Regiment, and Rogers captain of its ranging company number one. (I. N. Phelps Strokes Collection, Miriam and Ira D. Wallach Division of Art, Prints and Photographs, The New York Public Library, Astor, Lenox and Tilden Foundations)

were the men serving in the single company he commanded. By courtesy, the title was extended to the other ranger companies (excepting provincial units) with the Hudson valley/Lake George army, since he was the senior ranger officer there.

Rogers first captained ranger company number one of Colonel Joseph Blanchard's New Hampshire Regiment in the 1755 Lake George campaign. Thirty-two hardy souls volunteered to remain with him at Fort William Henry that winter to continue scouting and raiding the enemy forts in the north, despite the non-availability of bounty or salary money.

Near the beginning of the spring of 1756, reports of Rogers' success in the field prompted Massachusetts' Governor-General William Shirley (then temporary commander of British forces) to award him "the command of an independent company of rangers," to consist of 60 privates, three sergeants, an ensign and two lieutenants. Robert's brother, Richard, would be his first lieutenant. No longer on a provincial footing, Rogers' rangers would be paid and fed out of the royal war chest and answerable to British commanders. Although not on a permanent establishment, ranger officers would receive almost the same pay as redcoat officers, while ranger privates would earn twice as much as their provincial counterparts, who were themselves paid higher wages than the regulars. (Captain Joseph Gorham's older ranger company, based in Nova Scotia, enjoyed a royal commission, and thus a permanency denied those units serving in the Hudson valley.)

The frontiersmen

Rogers was ordered by Shirley "to inlist none but such as were used to travelling and hunting, and in whose courage and fidelity I could confide." The frontier towns of New Hampshire's Merrimack valley bred such men, and in the spring many of them gathered at Amoskeag Falls to harvest the running shad and salmon. A typical young frontier farmer from nearby Derryfield, while working his net in the foamy waters that April of 1756, would have seen Robert and Richard Rogers appear on the riverbank, carrying orders to recruit their company "as quick as possible."

He would have listened as they appealed to his patriotism, spoke glowingly of a ranger private's daily pay of three shillings New York currency, and showed him the ten Spanish dollars bounty "allowed to each man towards providing cloaths, arms, and blankets." In addition there was the enticement of £5 sterling for each scalp or prisoner taken. (In Nova Scotia in 1757 the bounties were raised to £25 and £30,

A modern re-enactor in the uniform of the ranger companies at Nova Scotia (including those of captains Joseph Gorham and James Rogers) in 1759.
A sleeved waistcoat was worn under a black, sleeveless jacket with shoulder wings. Extra warmth was provided by a blue, kilt-like petticoat. The leggings buttoned from the calf downward. (Author's photo)

respectively.) By signing up he would help quicken the inevitable fall of New France, which would both end the Indian raids on the frontier towns and open up the vast Abenaki hunting grounds to settlement, including sizable land grants for war veterans.

If the Derryfield farmer was typical of most early ranger recruits, he would have been of Scots-Irish descent – that is, his parents had emigrated to America from the Lowland Scots communities of Ulster Plantation (Northern Ireland). Religious bigotry in Boston and other colonial cities had forced most of the Presbyterian Scots-Irish to settle on the frontier, where they acted as a handy buffer against French and Indian raids. They were a lively people, "more frank and rough in their manners" than the English, as one early New Hampshire historian put it. They were fond of practical jokes, rum, wrestling, gaming, and filing lawsuits. Heavy debt was common, and some, like Robert Rogers himself, were not above dabbling in such vices as passing counterfeit bills.

If the Derryfield farmer was a typical ranger prospect, he would have had little better than a rudimentary frontier education. Physically he might have resembled the three deserters from Captain John Stark's 1759 company, who were described as "all lusty, stout men, six feet [1.8m] high." (Rogers himself was a six-footer, and said to be "a man of uncommon strength.") One correspondent with Amherst's Ticonderoga campaign deemed Rogers' rangers "hearty Fellows." Their frequently exacting service required that recruits be exceptionally tough as

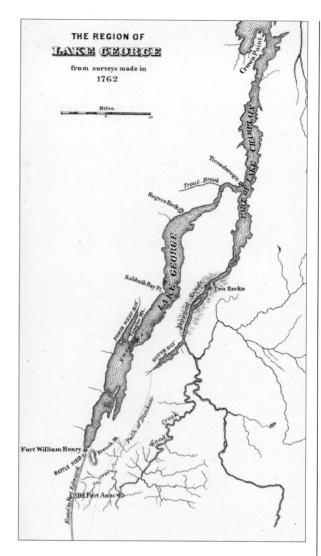

ABOVE **The primary battlefield of Rogers' rangers between 1755 and 1759: the rivers, lakes, islands, swamps, and forested mountains of the northern New York war front. (Author's collection)**

LEFT **The New Hampshire frontier provided some of the best rangers. Fast-loading during a hunt or an Indian fight was done by spitting bullets directly into the gun barrel. At Cherry Pond, Dennis Stanley shot down four moose in a row. (Author's drawing)**

well as brave; "Men of Constitutions like Lions," is how one New York newspaper described Rogers' corps.

When bringing their enlistment forms to the Merrimack valley towns, the Rogers brothers would have solicited recruits "by Beat of Drum or otherwise," as Lord Loudoun ordered Robert to do in 1758. In March 1759, ranger Captain Jonathan Brewer put an advertisement in a Boston newspaper announcing that "All Gentlemen Volunteers" wishing to join his company were to "repair to the captain's Quarters at the Sign of the Lamb at the South End of Boston, and enter into present Pay (which is nine Dollars and a half per Month) and good Quarters; and shall receive one Month's Advance." Taverns had an obvious advantage: recruiting expenses allowed the prospective ranger to be coaxed with mugs of flip, rum, or punch. The Articles of War were read to each recruit, who then swore the oath of fidelity to "his Majesty King George the Second," and signed a form binding him to a year's service (later recruits would engage for the duration of the war).

The availability of men in the frontier towns often depended on the time of the year. "The Season for the Beaver, which comes about the 20th February & continues three months," Rogers wrote to Loudoun in late 1756, "will much retard recruiting." On his spring recruiting drive that year he had managed to sign up 37 men, including John Stark as his

ABOVE **A copy of the only known life portrait of John Stark, sketched when the ex-ranger was about 82. Stark had been a captive of the St Francis Abenaki in his early trapping days. He served as an officer in Rogers' corps for four years, and became a major-general during the Revolution, stopping a British flank attack at Breed's Hill and in 1777 crushing Colonel Frederick Baum's force at Bennington. (Author's collection)**

LEFT **A model of Fort St Frederic at the Crown Point Visitors Center. The tall, massive "Citadel" had walls 10ft (3m) thick, its portholes mounting some 20 pieces of ordnance. Rogers sketched at least one plan of this fort from a nearby mountain. (Author's photo)**

MAJOR ROBERT ROGERS,
Commander in Chief of the INDIANS in the Back Settlements of AMERIC
Publish'd as the Act directs Oct'r 1776 by Tho's Hart.

Mezzotint "portrait" of Major Robert Rogers, published in London in 1776, a completely spurious likeness, unfortunately referenced in studies of ranger uniforms. In fact, the only authentic items seen were lifted from Benjamin West's *The Death of General Wolfe*. This print was made when it was still thought that Rogers, at the head of a detachment of Indian allies, had joined Washington's army. (Author's collection)

second lieutenant. In typical Rogers fashion he sent half his new recruits to Fort Edward on the Hudson, while he took the rest directly on their first raid near French-held Fort St Frederic, on Lake Champlain. That he was able to do this suggests the high caliber of these recruits. (Enough rangers of his winter company decided to re-enlist to meet the company requirement of 60 privates.) By July 1756, a second company was commissioned, with younger brother Richard Rogers its captain, and Robert becoming brevet major over both companies and all the other independent ranger units in the region.

Ranger recruits from the New Hampshire frontier were highly skilled outdoorsmen, long used to trapping beaver and muskrat, hunting deer, bear, catamount, moose and wolves, and surviving in various extremes of wilderness conditions. (Author's drawing)

The non-frontiersmen

The quality of men found in those ranger companies not personally recruited by Rogers or his officers was a notably variable one. Two companies raised by captains Thomas Speakman and Humphrey Hobbs in mid-1756 had few real woodsmen in their ranks. "The best of their Men," observed William Shirley, "[are] Irish Roman Catholicks, the others mostly Sailors and Spaniards." Many of them had been recruited along the Boston waterfront and in neighboring communities. One of the privates, Thomas Brown of Acton, was a 16-year-old apprentice laborer. The increasing dearth of true frontiersmen to fill up the ranks of the many new ranger companies raised during the war became a real problem. "You are to enlist no vagrants," Loudoun instructed Rogers upon the augmentation of his company to 100 men in early 1757. "If any [of the men] are found insufficient for the service the blame will be laid upon you." Some non-frontiersmen, like Harvard student Isaac Day and Boston's Benjamin Hutchins, proved themselves fine rangers; in 1759 Hutchins, now an ensign, carried a message from General Amherst across the Maine wilderness to General Wolfe on the St Lawrence. Private Emanuel la Portgua died fighting on snowshoes in Rogers' winter battle of January 1757.

TRAINING AND TACTICS

Because the men of Rogers' own company, and of those additional companies his veteran officers were assigned to raise, were generally frontier-bred, the amount of basic training they had to undergo was not as protracted as that endured by the average redcoat recruit. Our Derryfield farmer, for instance, would have entered the ranger service as an already proficient tracker and hunter. He was probably able to construct a bark or brush lean-to in less than an hour, find direction in the darkest woods, make rope from the inner bark of certain trees, and survive for days on a scanty trail diet.

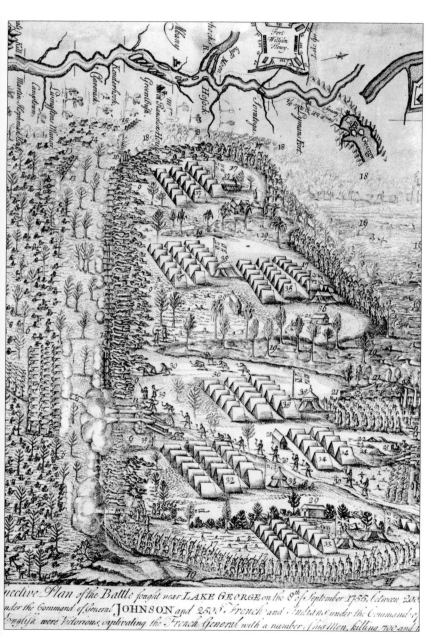

Another detail from Blodgett's 1755 Perspective Plan, showing how the victorious New England troops at Lake George engaged the attacking French and Indians by firing and loading in prone positions behind log breastworks. The aligned ranks of French regulars (left center) eventually broke apart, the soldiers taking cover behind brush and stumps like their partisan allies. (I. N. Phelps Strokes Collection, Miriam and Ira D. Wallach Division of Art, Prints and Photographs, The New York Public Library, Astor, Lenox and Tilden Foundations)

Marksmanship

The typical New Hampshire recruit could also "shoot amazingly well," as Captain Henry Pringle of the 27th Foot observed. Based at Fort Edward and a volunteer in one of Rogers' biggest scouting excursions, Pringle wrote in December 1757 of one ranger officer who, "the other day, at four shots with four balls, killed a brace of Deer, a Pheasant, and a pair of wild ducks – the latter he killed at one Shot." In fact, many New England troops, according to an eyewitness in Nova Scotia, could "load their firelocks upon their back, and then turn upon their bellies, and take aim at their enemies: There are no better marksmen in the world, for their whole delight is shooting at marks for wages."

The heavy emphasis on marksmanship in Rogers' corps, and the issuance of rifled carbines to many of the men, paid off in their frequent success against the Canadians and Indians. (Marksmanship remains among the most important of all ranger legacies, one that continues to be stressed in the training of today's high-tech special forces.) Even in Rogers' only large-scale defeat, the Battle on Snowshoes of 13 March 1758, the sharpshooting of his heavily outnumbered rangers held off the encircling enemy for 90 minutes. Over two dozen Indians alone were killed and wounded, among the dead one of their war chiefs. This was an unusually high casualty rate for the stealthy Native Americans ("who are not accustomed to lose," said Montcalm of the battle). So enraged were the Indians that they summarily executed a like number of rangers who had surrendered on the promise of good quarter.

Benjamin West's 1760 painting, *Savage Warrior Taking Leave of His Family*. Red feathers and ostrich plumes decorate his head. A scarlet stroud is wrapped around his waist, and his leggings are also scarlet. (Reproduced by kind permission of The President and Council of The Royal College of Surgeons of England)

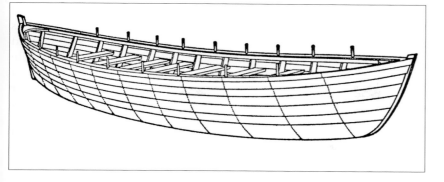

Bateaux were rowed by Rogers' men early in the war. "Stupid ... Clumsy worthless things," according to New Hampshire's Colonel Blanchard, they nevertheless transported the bulk of the main armies and their cargoes down rivers and across lakes. (Author's collection)

Other disciplines

Learning how to operate water craft on the northern lakes and streams was another crucial skill for every ranger. Birchbark canoes and bateaux (rowing vessels made for transporting goods) were used in Rogers' earliest forays on Lake George. In 1756, these were swapped for newly arrived whaleboats made of light cedar planking. Designed for speed, they had keels, round bottoms, and sharp ends, allowing for a quick change of direction and agile handling even on choppy waters. Blankets could be rigged as improvised sails.

Additional things the new recruit had to learn, or at least to perfect, included: how to build a raft, how to ford a rapid river without a raft or boat, how to portage a whaleboat over a mountain range, how to "log" a position in the forest as a makeshift breastwork, how to design and sew a pair of moccasins, how to utter bird and animal calls as "private signals" in the woods, and sometimes how to light and hurl a grenade.

Whaleboats became the rangers' watercraft of choice. Some had been brought to Lake George from Cape Cod and Nantucket; others were made at Fort William Henry from local cedar trees. When sneaking past the narrow strait at Crown Point in 1756, the oars of the ranger whaleboats "were bound with cloth." In 1758 and 1759, all the boats in the army had to be marked by regiment or company. (Author's drawing)

LEFT Rogers' rangers carried hand grenades (right) to attack French vessels on Lake Champlain, and in 1757 burned the enemy's cordwood piles and a storehouse outside Fort Carillon with "fireballs." Left: a "carcass," a parchment-covered iron framework loaded with gunpowder and other combustibles, and sometimes bristling with hooks. In 1759, rangers attempted to sink a French ship by swimming out to her with "fire-darts and hand-carcasses." (Author's collection)

BELOW A provincial soldier on temporary ranger duty near Crown Point in 1760. Provincial clothing and equipment lists often included leggings, moccasins, tumplines, and tomahawks. (Author's painting)

Provincial draftees

Threatened by a possible invasion from Montcalm's forces in the north, and with Rogers' companies dispatched to Nova Scotia, General Daniel Webb in the summer of 1757 directed that six temporary ranger companies be drafted from the provincial regiments at Fort Edward. Cartridge boxes were laid aside, and the men were issued "Leather Shot Bags and Powder Horns." The results were mixed, yet promising enough for Lord Loudoun to contemplate raising more such companies later that year. Some of the provincials pointed out that they lacked "Blanketts, Indian Shoes, Indian Stockings, and proper Coats, all which is absolutely Necessary should [they] act as Rangers." Yet so great was the need for more Anglo-American irregulars that those provincials "willing & fit to serve with Major Rogers" in 1758 were offered "an encouragement over and above their present pay." Under his personal leadership these soldiers learned fast and performed well. On one expedition in the deep forest, for instance, Connecticut draftee Abel Spicer was taught the importance of countersigns: "if you hailed anybody and they did not answer Boston, you must take them to be an enemy." Provincials volunteering to serve with Rogers in 1759 were ordered "not to take

their tents but live in Huts, in the same manner as the Rangers do [and to] draw their Provisions with the Rangers."

Training the regulars

In 1756, a detail of New Hampshire provincial rangers was sent to Saratoga "to instruct the Regulars in scouting, building camps, and in short in making war after the New england fashion." That same year also saw a few ambitious regulars, like Lieutenant Quinton Kennedy and cadet Henry Marr of the 44th Foot, attempt to lead scouting parties into enemy country, with disastrous results. Other redcoats, such as Lord Howe, volunteer Ronald Chalmers, Captain James Abercrombie of the 42nd Highlanders, and Captain Thomas Davies of the Royal Artillery, fared better because they chose to be educated in the field by Rogers himself. Another regular, Colonel George Prevost of the 60th Foot (the Royal Americans), recommended in 1757 that his regiment be allowed to adopt field attire and weapons not unlike Rogers' corps, and that each man "should be trained to fire blanks in all kinds of situations, to walk on snowshoes, run, jump, swim, obey a whistle … [and] be capable of constructing and driving the boats and canoes necessary for navigating the lakes."

Because the modus operandi of rangers remained unknown to the bulk of the regular army, Rogers was ordered by Loudoun in 1757 to pen a compendium of "rules, or plan of discipline," for those "Gentlemen Officers" who wanted to learn ranger methods. To ensure that the lessons were properly understood, 50 regular volunteers from eight regiments formed a special company to fall under Rogers' tutelage. His job was to instruct them in "our methods of marching, retreating, ambushing, fighting, &c." Many of these rules, totaling 28 in number, were essentially derived from old Indian tactics and techniques, and were well known to New England frontiersmen.

Rule II, for instance, specified that if your scouting party is small, "march in a single file, keeping at such a distance from each other as to prevent one shot from killing two men." Rule V recommended that a party leaving enemy country should return home by a different route, to avoid

LEFT Brigadier-General George Augustus, 3rd Viscount Howe, who went scouting with Rogers and Stark to Ticonderoga and eagerly adopted ranger ways. Killed in a bush fight two days before the assault on Fort Carillon, "his fall was most sincerely lamented," wrote Rogers. (Author's collection)

BELOW A "rangerized" soldier of Lord Howe's 55th Regiment of Foot in 1758. A shortened coat, checked shirt, "Indian stockings," moccasins, tumpline pack, trimmed hair and hat, and tomahawk make him ready for woods service. "You would laugh to see the droll Figure we all cut," one of the redcoats wrote to a friend. "You would not distinguish us from common Ploughmen." (Author's drawing)

CURRENT

How Rogers' rangers crossed the rapid St Francis River: Wrote Rogers: "I put the tallest men upstream [i.e., facing the current], and then holding by each other, we got over." This technique required the line of men to move in a side-step fashion. Most clothing had been removed to facilitate movement and to avoid having to build fires to dry out afterwards. (Author's diagram)

being ambushed on its own tracks. Rule X warned that if the enemy was about to overwhelm you, "let the whole body disperse, and every one take a different road to the place of rendezvous appointed for the evening."

Other rules required that even the most proficient New Hampshire recruit had to undergo special training in bush fighting tactics. If 300 to 400 rangers were marching "with a design to attack the enemy," noted Rule VI, "divide your party into three columns . . . and let the columns march in single files, the columns to the right and left keeping at twenty yards [20m] distance or more from that of the center," with proper guards in front, rear, and on the flanks. If attacked in front, "form a front of your three columns or main body with the advanced guard, keeping out your flanking parties … to prevent the enemy from pursuing hard on either of your wings, or surrounding you, which is the usual method of the savages."

Rule VII advised the rangers to "fall, or squat down," if forced to take the enemy's first fire, and "then rise and discharge at them." Rule IX suggested that "if you are obliged to retreat, let the front of your whole party fire and fall back, till the rear hath done the same, making for the best ground you can, by this means you will oblige the enemy to pursue you, if they do it at all, in the face of a constant fire."

Such large-scale tactics were sometimes staged by the rangers for the edification of the rest of the army as well as for their own benefit. For instance, nine days after Rogers' defeat of Canadian partisan Joseph Marin in August 1758, "a great Number" of the regulars and provincials in Abercromby's camp "Took a Walk to the Great Plain to View Major Rogers & the Rangers Exercising their method thay took when they had their fight at the South Bay & in what manner the Indians generally

Three regulars training in a swamp in 1758 replenish their canteens. The man at far right adds powdered ginger to his water, which was thought to prevent scurvy, the "bloody flux" (dysentery), and ague. Their muskets have been sawed down, and the barrels blackened to kill reflections. The meal they carried was mixed with water and baked "in cakes, by putting it on a flat stone under the ashes." (Author's drawing)

Manage in their Battles." Two days later, the general himself "and several of the chief officers" went to observe a second demonstration.

The rangers' example not only led to practical renovations in the dress, arms, accouterments, and tactics of the regulars, but also inspired the formation of the first regiment of British light infantry, the 80th, under Colonel Thomas Gage. Although never relied upon as scouts or commandos the way Rogers' companies were, elements of the 80th served well under his field leadership, especially at Fort Anne in 1758 and on the St Francis expedition in 1759.

Miscellaneous ranger tactics

Most of Rogers' activities during the war, however, consisted not of battles and skirmishes but of lightning raids, pursuits, and other special operations. As General Shirley's 1756 orders stated, Rogers was "to use my best endeavours to distress the French and their allies, by sacking, burning, and destroying their houses, barns, barracks, canoes, battoes, &c." The "&c" included slaughtering the enemy's herds of cattle and horses, ambushing and destroying his provision sleighs, setting fire to his fields of grain and piles of cordwood, sneaking into the ditches of his forts to make observations, and seizing prisoners for interrogation. One French grenadier on sentry duty outside Fort Carillon mistook a casually approaching Rogers for a Canadian until the latter replied "Rogers" to his question, "Qui êtes vous?" The rangers hurried him back to their base, after "cutting his breeches and coat from him, that he might march with the greater ease and expedition."

Captain Thomas Davies' *A South West View of the Lines and Fort of Tyconderoga*, as drawn in 1759 after Amherst's capture. The view is from the summit of Rattlesnake Mountain – the same vantage point Rogers' rangers had used to study enemy activity at the fort over the previous four years. (Thomas Davies, National Archives of Canada/C-010653)

At least one British commander, General Abercromby, frowned on the ranger practice of shooting guns in the woods beyond the camp in order to lure the enemy into a fight. Sometimes rangers would disguise themselves as fishermen on the lakes, acting as decoys to draw out French and Indian parties. Rogers was also said to have donned Indian dress – probably including facial paint – in order to walk through the village of St Francis the night before he attacked it, "and was spoken to several Times by the Indians but was not discovered."

When a British sleigh train was attacked near Fort Edward in early March 1758, Rogers "and a Number of his Men, with Snow Shoes, Arms, and Ammunition, most of them stripped to their Shirts, were out of Sight" of Fort Edward less than 15 minutes after the alarm came in.

While General Abercromby's assaulting redcoats were being decimated in the great abatis in front of Fort Carillon in July 1758, Rogers and his rangers kept hidden within the mesh of fallen trees, sniping at the embrasures in the French breastworks. (Captain Louis Antoine de Bougainville, who suffered a head wound, noted that these marksmen "delivered a most murderous fire on us.")

When the French garrison at Ticonderoga was discovered evacuating their fort under cover of night in 1759, General Amherst ordered Rogers and his rangers to try to head them off in their whaleboats. Precious minutes were expended as Rogers sawed apart a boom lying across the strait; once through, his waterborne column swept on, corralling ten enemy boats liberally stocked with ammunition, gunpowder, official papers, and prisoners.

In 1760, Rogers captured Fort St Therese on the Richelieu River by waiting until a hay cart was just entering the gateway. His rangers, with a contingent of light infantry, dashed from their cover and poured into the fort, seizing it while another body of his men was simultaneously capturing the adjacent village, all "without firing a single shot."

Tactics employed by Captain James Smith on the Pennsylvania frontier during Pontiac's War were largely familiar to Rogers. For instance, Smith would assign every two of his rangers "to take a tree … with orders to keep a reserve fire, one not to fire until his comrade had loaded his gun – by this means we kept up a constant, slow fire." Once a captive of the Indians, Smith wrote a treatise on their manner of fighting, and asked the questions: "Why have we not made greater proficiency in the Indian art of war? Is it because we are too proud to imitate them, even though it should be a means of preserving the lives of many of our citizens?"

On 31 July 1763, Captain James Dalyell of the 1st Regiment of Foot endeavored to show that the approach of frontiersmen like Smith was wrong, that regular discipline and tactics were superior to those of Native Americans. He led a column of 297 men, mostly regulars, out of

Plan of Abercromby's attack against the French lines outside Fort Carillon on 8 July 1758. "Ye New Ingland men kept behind trees and logs as much as they could," wrote one provincial, "but ye regalars kept so nigh and in plain sight that ye French cut them down amazin." (Author's collection)

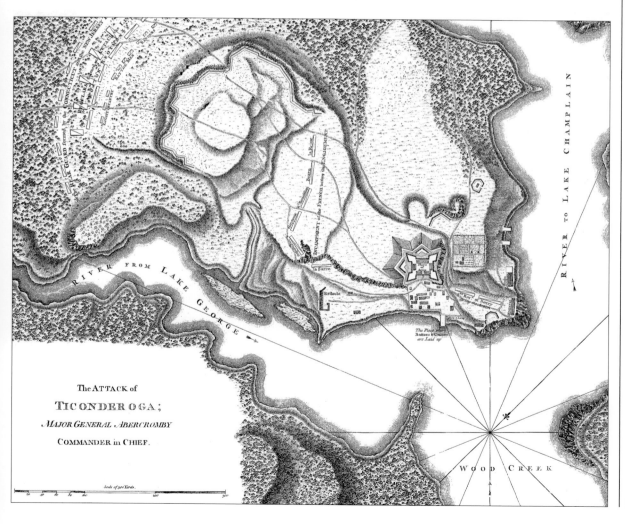

The ATTACK of
TICONDEROGA;
MAJOR GENERAL ABERCROMBY
COMMANDER in CHIEF.

Scale of 300 Yards.

Fort Detroit to engage Pontiac's warriors with fixed bayonets. Robert Rogers came along, but this time in a subordinate role. Dalyell, who had fought alongside Rogers at Fort Anne in 1758, had evidently forgotten those earlier lessons in bush fighting. Instead his men, in parade formation, walked into an ambush; dozens fell as they responded in street-firing volleys. Dalyell eventually ordered a retreat, but was himself soon killed. Now Rogers took over, instructing the regulars to stop shooting in platoons, abandon their exposed positions, and make their way back to the fort by hopping from house to house along the road. The tactic saved the column from annihilation, as the regulars themselves later acknowledged. Yet sadly, it was not until World War Two that such unorthodox – and sensible – fighting methods would become the universal military standard.

CAMP LIFE

Wherever Rogers' companies made their camp, it was not with tents, but with bark shelters or log huts, depending on the length of time they were to remain there. The men of the New Hampshire Regiment in 1755 were "very expert [at building] Bark Houses," noted a New York official, "& when they decamp roll up the Bark & carry with them." A huge blockhouse built on Rogers' Island as their barracks was rejected by the rangers, who preferred to live in cozier, better-heated log huts.

ABOVE **Tiyanoga, or Hendrick, a Mohawk chief killed at the battle of Lake George. The Mohawks proved invaluable allies mainly because they knew the country in which the rangers had to scout. Rogers praised his Iroquois contingent for their service during his action against French and Indians near Ticonderoga in March 1759. (Author's collection)**

RIGHT **A simple "shed" of bark sheets on a framework of poles, called an encampment by the French. In his** *A Concise Account of North America*, **Rogers noted that such "Indian hunting-houses are generally but the work of half an hour at the most." (Author's drawing)**

Camp duties

When encamped with the main army, the rangers' duties included making daily patrols beyond the perimeter, guarding workers on the road and in the woods, rounding up stray cattle, carrying mail and messages to other posts, apprehending deserters, and sometimes escorting provision wagon trains. Their status as a special force generally freed them from most of the drudge work of a typical military campaign, such as fort building, ditch digging, and rowing and poling supply boats. But the regular commanders invariably thought up ways to utilize their special skills. At Fort Edward in February 1758, "a Number of Majr Rogerss men," wrote a provincial diarist, "was over On this Side with their Snow Shoes to Tread Down ye Snow Round on the Glassea [glacis]." In 1759, General Amherst ordered the rangers to help hack out two roads, one of them 77 miles (124km) long and connecting

Captain Thomas Davies' *View of the Lines at Lake George*, 1759. Amherst's camp is in middleground, the Lake George no-man's land beyond. (Fort Ticonderoga Museum)

RIGHT **Davies' *A South View of the New Fortress at Crown Point ... in the Year 1759*. Amherst's huge fort is marked "A," the ruins of Fort St Frederic marked "B." (Courtesy Winterthur Museum)**

BELOW **The Rogers' Island/Fort Edward complex as it probably looked in the fall of 1757. The ranger hut camp is in foreground. Around the fort extends an outerwork protecting tent camps of regular and provincial troops. (Author's drawing)**

Crown Point to the distant Connecticut River. He also "sent Mr Rogers on the other side the Lake to see for the best Place for cutting timber to erect the Fort." In Nova Scotia in 1757, Rogers wrote that some of his men had to "cut and make up hay in the meadows, for the horses intended to be used in an expedition to Louisbourg" – work our Derryfield farmer was very familiar with.

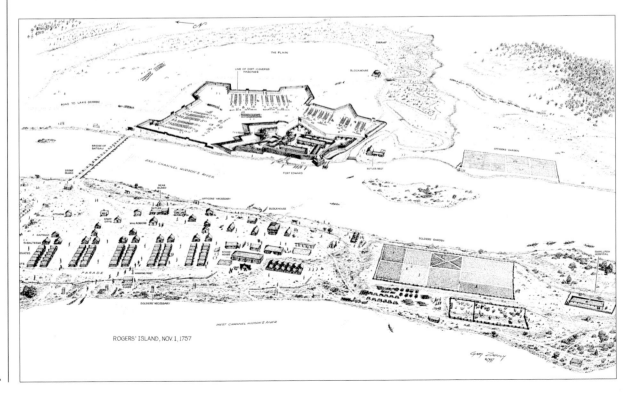

ROGERS' ISLAND, NOV. 1, 1757

Camp diet

Ranger hunters brought in fresh game for food and hides. But the recruit soon discovered that most of his camp meals consisted of salt pork and beef, hard sea biscuits, or rice cooked with butter. At times this fare was supplemented with fish, peas, cheese, and cakes of chocolate (the latter boiled into a beverage). Flour was occasionally provided for baking bread. Rum was usually doled out to each ranger at a gill (quarter pint) a day. Sometimes cider was available; at other times the men brought in spruce branches to brew and ferment with molasses. The end result, "spruce beer," was considered an antiscorbutic as well as liquor. Officers could afford more elegant spirits such as brandy and Madeira wine. On Rogers' Island, in the Hudson next to Fort Edward, the log-hutted rangers dined on greasy puncheon tables, their forks and knives made of pewter or lead, their plates and cups of tin.

Off-duty life

Conversation over clay pipes, chewing tobacco, and snuff helped while away the rare hours of leisure, as did impromptu singing or concerts with fiddle and jew's harp. Cards, dice, and draughts, sometimes played for money or rum, kept the smoke-filled huts boisterous. Newspapers and books made the rounds, but few of the men did much writing: ranger diaries and letters are very rare. Now and then there was a wrestling match, or an angry fistfight. The men had to do their own laundry: a practice Lord Howe ordered his regular officers to emulate in 1758. In January of that year, the Hudson River rose so high that it flooded the huts on Rogers' Island, some of them "Waist Deep in Water," and washed away precious stacks of firewood.

Detail from Captain Thomas Davies' *A South View of ... Crown Point*. **"Hutts of Rangers & Indians Wigwams" are shown, according to the key. Bark lodges can be seen near the log huts in several forms: wigwam, tent, and lean-to. (Thomas Davies, National Archives of Canada /C-013314)**

Women allowed at the northern outposts consisted of soldiers' wives and camp followers. The latter sometimes underwent a physical "to Examen Whether they Had the &c. or Not," as a provincial at Fort Edward obliquely noted in 1757. Rangers on furlough in Albany leered at the Dutch girls who often worked with overskirts pulled up to their hips, revealing "the greater part of ye Leg." Some rangers may even have taken Indian wives: not such an exotic thing when one considers that Quinton Kennedy and Charles Lee, both regular officers, married Mohawk women.

One unique craft many rangers were adept at was making snowshoes. In early 1758, Rogers' men were assigned the job of producing several hundred pairs for a winter expedition against Fort Carillon planned by the regulars. Skinners had to dress the deer hides by steeping them overnight in water and then scraping off the hair. From these, thongs were cut, and laced and netted to hickory branches that had been bent and lashed into hoops. The rangers also had to teach the redcoats how to walk with them.

Camp regulations

In his Rule I, Rogers instructed that every evening all rangers were to "appear at roll-call … on their own parade, equipped, each with a fire-lock, sixty rounds of powder and ball, and a hatchet, at which time an officer from each company is to inspect the same, to see they are in order, so as to be ready on any emergency to march at a minute's warning." Before dismissal the night guards were picked, along with scouting parties for the following day.

At a sudden crisis the officers would shout, "Turn out, rangers!" and the men would rush to their parades with arms in hand. A sergeant and a squad of privates were rotated to keep watch over the guardhouse and its prisoners. Although it was rarely used, a whipping post stood on the rangers' parade ground on the island. Every evening the bottoms of the holes in their riverbank "necessary houses" were covered with "fresh earth."

Powder horn of Stockbridge Indian captain Jacob Cheeksaunkun, engraved at Fort William Henry. (Collection of the Fort Ticonderoga Museum)

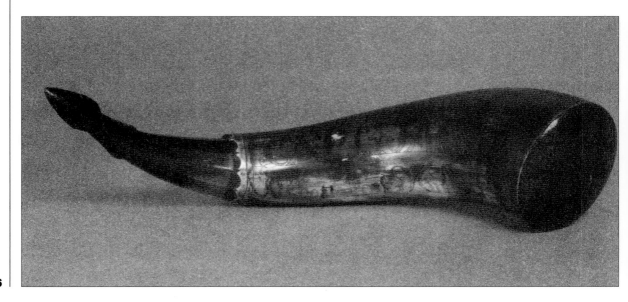

Robert Rogers and Captain Jacob Cheeksaunkun scout ahead of Amherst's advanced guard of rangers and light infantry as it approaches the southern end of Lake George in June 1759. The road from Fort Edward, cut in 1755, had witnessed numerous bloody ambushes. (Author's painting)

A company of Stockbridge Indians arrived at Rogers' Island in the summer of 1756 and encamped themselves near the huts of the white rangers. They enjoyed the same pay scale as the latter, although sutlers were "strictly forbid to give or sell rum" to them. To remain identifiable as English-friendly Indians, they had "a red garter fix'd at the muzzle of their guns when they come near any of our posts," wrote a regular orderly in 1758. Nervous provincials and regulars on guard duty sometimes mistook Rogers' white rangers, who "dress and live like the Indians" (according to Captain Henry Pringle), for enemy warriors. On a few occasions faulty countersign exchanges resulted in returning rangers getting wounded, or even killed.

Health

Scurvy closely nipped at the rangers' heels. It was not always easy to keep troops in winter quarters supplied with sufficient quantities of spruce beer, or "Turnips and other Greens," as Lord Loudoun advised, and for a ranger on a long scouting trek it was impossible. Rogers himself underwent a month-long bout of the disease in late 1757. Smallpox, too, could often sweep through an entire company, and a special hospital for sufferers was constructed at the isolated southern end of Rogers' Island. (Robert's brother Richard died of the disease at Fort William Henry.) Some rangers, like John Stark, had legs occasionally afflicted with the "hunter's lameness" (rheumatism). Accidents such as being crushed to death or severely injured by falling trees were common. Peter Bowen, of Rogers' company, lost an eye from a fellow ranger's musket being discharged during an exercise. One canoe split open on stormy Lake Champlain in 1760, drowning eight rangers.

ON CAMPAIGN

When the big armies under Johnson, Abercromby, Forbes, Wolfe, Amherst, Bouquet, and others marched into enemy territory, rangers acted as advanced and flank guards, often engaging and repulsing the kind of partisan attacks that had destroyed Braddock's force. One imperative in bush fighting was camouflage; for Rogers' men, green attire was a constant throughout the war. Other Anglo-American irregulars, like Gage's 80th Light Infantry and Putnam's Connecticut rangers, wore brown. Some, like Bradstreet's armed bateau men and Dunn's New Jersey rangers, wore gray. A few ranger companies in Nova Scotia wore dark blue or black.

Uniforms and field dress

Green may have been their color of choice, but Rogers' men never enjoyed a consistent uniform pattern throughout their five-year career, as the regulars and some provincial regiments did. On campaign with Rogers in Nova Scotia in July 1757, the Derryfield farmer-turned-ranger would have been dressed in "no particular uniform," according to observer Captain John Knox of the 46th, who added that each ranger wore his "cloaths short." This probably signified a variety of coats, jackets, waistcoats, or just shirts, all deliberately trimmed to make them lighter.

In the field, the rangers often resembled Indians, exhibiting a "cut-throat, savage appearance," as one writer at Louisbourg recorded in 1758. For the drive against Fort Duquesne that same year, General John Forbes encouraged his provincials to wear Indian dress. Massachusetts soldier Rufus Putnam, doing temporary duty as a ranger in 1757, complained of camping one night in the woods east of Lake George, bedeviled by "the gnats and mosquitoes … having no blankets; and I had nothing but a shirt and Indian stockings, and no man can tell what an affliction those little animals were." Another provincial party that summer was led by General Phineas Lyman, who went "painted like a Mohog [Mohawk] as many other officers of ye Scout were." Captain John Stark's account book for 1759 lists purchases of an "Indian flap,"

Powder horn of Robert Rogers dated "June ye 3rd, 1756," its carving attributed to John Bush, a free black Massachusetts provincial who also decorated other horns during the war. (Collection of the Fort Ticonderoga Museum)

or breechcloth, for 2 shillings, "Indian Stockings" for 12 shillings, and a "tumpline" for 4 shillings.

To Highland captain James Abercrombie, Rogers' rangers, despite their sometimes wild exterior, looked the very essence of true soldiers. "I was so pleased with their appearance when I was out with them," he wrote the major in February 1757, "that I took it for granted they would behave well whenever they met the enemy."

Ordered to raise five new ranger companies in January 1758, Rogers contracted that four of them were to receive clothing made "chiefly of Green Bath Rug & low priced green Cloths with wt. [white] Mettle Buttons & white Silver lace Hats, some of them Silver laced, cord or looping on their Jackets, all lin'd with Green Serge." (The occasions

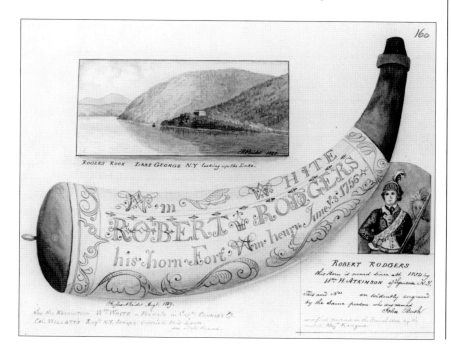

An 1889 rendering of Rogers' powder horn. Note insert of Rogers' Rock, site of Rogers' legendary and spectacular escape from Indians in March 1758. (Collection of The New-York Historical Society)

Detail of Captain Thomas Davies' *View of the Lines at Lake George, 1759*. The foreground figures are unidentified, but the reclining Indian is probably one of the Stockbridge scouts, and the green-clad white man may represent a ranger, perhaps even Robert Rogers himself. (Fort Ticonderoga Museum)

when Rogers' men wore such uniforms, rather than Indian costume – or perhaps even a mix of both – obviously depended on the nature of their assignments.) This order marked one of the few times that several of his companies were commonly uniformed, but only one of the new companies, composed of Mohegan Indians (who were ordered to be "dressed in all respects in the true Indian fashion"), went to join him on Rogers' Island, the other four being sent directly to Halifax. His older companies had to make do with what apparel they could buy in the regimental stores at Fort Edward, or in Albany. The blockhouse of Captain Durkee of the provincials, for instance, offered "flaning [flannel] shurts shoes stockings mild [milled] caps and many larg pieses of Cloath cheefly striped and Checkd Flaning." An Albany-based agent for a New York clothier in April 1758 advised his employer that "I believe a parcel of Scotch Bonnets would sell well, as the Rangers who can get them wear nothing else when they go out."

In 1756, Gorham's ranger company at Chignecto, temporarily lacking a uniform, had to make do with "French prize Clothing."

Winter campaigning

Among the many perils facing a ranger assigned to a winter scout in the Adirondack Mountains were temperatures sometimes reaching 40 degrees below zero, snowblindness, bleeding feet, hypothermia, frostbite, gangrene, and lost fingers, toes, and noses. Deep slush often layered the frozen lakes, and sometimes a man would fall through a hole in the ice. Rogers routinely sent back those who began limping or complaining during the first days on the trail. Things only got more onerous as they neared the enemy forts: fireless camps had to be endured, unless they found a depression on a high ridge where a deep hole could be scooped out with snowshoes to accommodate a small fire. Around this were arrayed shelters of pine boughs, each containing "mattresses" of evergreen branches overlaid with bearskins. Wrapped in their blankets like human cocoons, the rangers would dangle their feet over the flames or coals to spend a tolerably comfortable night.

Guarding the ranger camp in no-man's land or enemy country required sentry parties numbering six men each, "two of whom must be constantly alert," noted Rogers, "and when relieved by their fellows, it should be done without noise." When dawn broke, the entire detachment was awakened, "that being the time when the savages chuse to fall upon their enemies." Before setting out again, the area around the campsite was probed for enemy tracks.

Drawing provisions, bedding, and extra clothing on hand-sleds prevented the men from burning too many calories and exuding dangerously excessive sweat. Expert snowshoers, they could nimbly climb "over several large mountains" in one day, as provincial Jeduthan Baldwin did on a trek with Rogers in March 1756. Aside from additional warm wear such as flannel under jackets, woolen socks, shoepack liners, fur caps, and thick mittens, the marching winter rangers wore their blankets wrapped, belted, and sometimes hooded around them, much as the Indians did.

"Bush tents of pine boughs" built around a "great fire," or a fire in a snow pit, served the rangers as shelters on winter scouts. (Author's drawing)

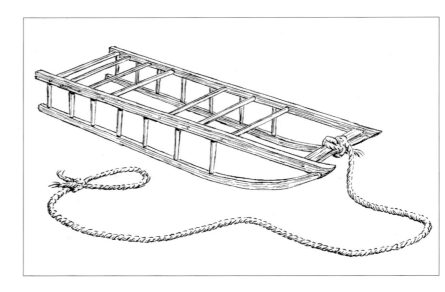

"One Hand Slay is Supposed to be provided for three Men who Draw it by Turns," wrote Lord Loudoun in September 1757 as he began planning a winter expedition against Ticonderoga. The all-wooden hand-sleds also carried packs, firewood, game, and wounded men. (Author's drawing)

Battling the French and Indians in snow that was often chest-deep could be lethal for a ranger with a broken snowshoe. Ironically, the green clothing worn by Rogers' men proved a liability when they had a white slope of snow behind them. According to Captain Pringle, during the 1758 Battle on Snowshoes, Rogers' servant was forced to lay "aside his green jacket in the field, as I did likewise my furred Cap, which became a mark to the enemy, and probably was the cause of a slight wound in my face." Pringle, "unaccustomed to Snow-Shoes," found himself unable to join the surviving rangers in their retreat at battle's end. He and two other men endured seven days of wandering the white forest before surrendering to the French.

Trail food and emergency subsistence
In January 1756, Captain John Rutherford of a New York independent company informed Lord Loudoun that the rangers at Lake George usually packed for the trail "Beef Pork Rum Sugar Rice and Peas" (the sugar possibly used to sweeten boiled chocolate). Their canteens carried rum, which was stretched with water while on the trail. On a winter trek in 1759, ranger sutler James Gordon wrote, "I had a pound or two of bread, a dozen crackers, about two [pounds of] fresh pork and a quart of brandy." Henry Pringle survived his post-battle ordeal in the forest by subsisting on "a small Bologna sausage, and a little ginger … water, & the bark & berries of trees." Rangers landing near Louisbourg on 8 June 1758 carried cheese and bread in their pockets.

Also eaten was the Indians' favorite trail food, parched corn – corn that had been parched and then pounded into flour. It was in effect an appetite suppressant: a spoonful of it, followed by a drink of water, expanded in the stomach, making the traveler feel he had consumed a large meal.

A mess of up to 15 rangers could be serviced by a small kettle. Toted eating utensils were simple: tin spoon, plate, and cup, aside from the scalping knife. Some men carried a combination clasp knife and fork, or the kind of sheathed fork and knife set that Lord Howe distributed to his officers. Provisions were usually stuffed into bags, *(continued on page 41)*

Private, Captain John Lovewell's New England Ranger Company, 1725

A

B

Recruitment and Training: Firing at marks, Fort William Henry, 1756

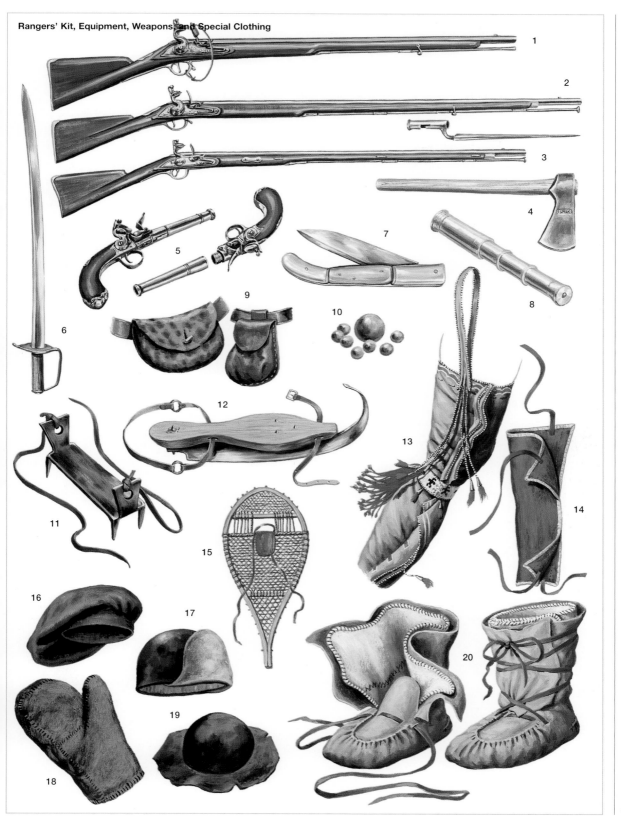

Rangers' Kit, Equipment, Weapons, and Special Clothing

C

Tactics and Combat Techniques: Ranger Defense Perimeter, La Barbue Creek, 1757

D

Daily Life: Rogers' Island, Spring 1758

E

F

After the Battle near Old Fort Anne, August 1758

Frontier Rangers, Pontiac's War, 1763-64

H

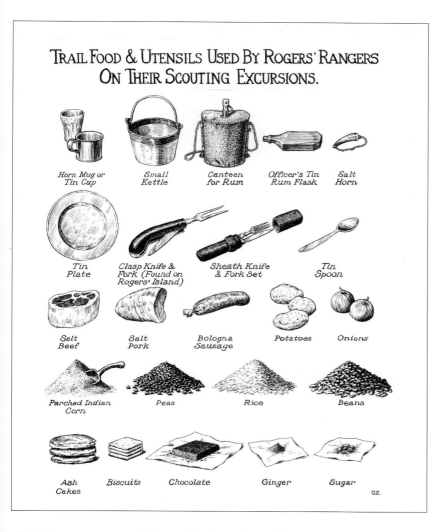

TRAIL FOOD & UTENSILS USED BY ROGERS' RANGERS ON THEIR SCOUTING EXCURSIONS.

Horn Mug or Tin Cup — Small Kettle — Canteen for Rum — Officer's Tin Rum Flask — Salt Horn

Tin Plate — Clasp Knife & Fork (Found on Rogers' Island) — Sheath Knife & Fork Set — Tin Spoon

Salt Beef — Salt Pork — Bologna Sausage — Potatoes — Onions

Parched Indian Corn — Peas — Rice — Beans

Ash Cakes — Biscuits — Chocolate — Ginger — Sugar

GZ.

which in turn were either rolled up in a blanket-tumpline pack, or carried in a knapsack.

Obtaining food from the enemy helped sustain rangers on their return home. Slaughtered cattle herds at Ticonderoga and Crown Point provided tongues ("a very great refreshment," noted Rogers). David Perry and several other rangers of Captain Moses Hazen's company raided a French house near Quebec in 1759, finding "plenty of pickled Salmon, which was quite a rarity to most of us." In another house they dined on "hasty-pudding." At St Francis, Rogers' men packed corn for the long march back, but after eight days, he wrote, their "provisions grew scarce." For some reason game was also scarce in the northern New England wilderness that fall of 1759, and the rangers' survival skills underwent severe tests even as they were being pursued by a vengeful enemy. Now and then they found an owl, partridge, or muskrat to shoot, but much of the time they dined on amphibians, mushrooms, beech leaves, and tree bark. Volunteer Robert Kirk of the 77th Highland Regiment wrote that "we were obliged to scrape under the snow for acorns, and even to eat our shoes and belts, and broil our powder-horns and thought it delicious eating."

During the long, hungry retreat from St Francis, a rare moment of grace occurred when Captain Joseph Waite's squad killed a deer. After consuming part of it, they left the remainder hanging from a tree for other parties expected that way. Waite carved his name on the tree in case an enemy trick was suspected. (Author's drawing)

Things grew so desperate that some rangers roasted Abenaki bounty scalps for the little circles of flesh they held. One small party of rangers and light infantry was ambushed and almost entirely destroyed by the French and Indians. When other rangers discovered the bodies, "on them, accordingly, they fell like Cannibals, and devoured part of them raw," stuffing the remaining flesh, including heads, into their packs. One ranger later confessed that he and his starving comrades "hardly deserved the name of human beings."

Other campaign challenges

"We are in a most damnable country," wrote a lieutenant of the 55th Foot at Lake George in 1758, "fit only for wolves, and its native savages." In such a demanding environment the rangers were constantly being pushed to their physical and psychological limits, especially when captives of the enemy. Teenager Thomas Brown, bleeding profusely from three bullet holes after Rogers' January 1757 battle near Ticonderoga, "concluded, if possible, to crawl into the Woods and there die of my Wounds." Taken prisoner by Indians, who often threatened his life, he was forced to dance around a fellow ranger who was being slowly tortured at a stake. Recovering from his wounds, Brown was later traded to a Canadian merchant, with whom he "fared no better than a Slave," before making his escape. Captain Israel Putnam himself was once saved from a burning stake by the last-minute intervention of a Canadian officer. Ranger William Moore had the heart of a slain comrade forced into his mouth. Later, he had some 200 pine splints stuck into his body,

each one about to be set afire by his captors, when a woman of the tribe announced she would adopt him. Two captured Indian rangers were shackled with irons and shipped to France, where they were sold into "extreme hard labour."

Tasks that might appear Herculean to others were strictly rote for the rangers. In July 1756, Rogers and his men chopped open a 6-mile (10km) path across the forested mountains between Lake George and Wood Creek, then hauled five armed whaleboats over it to make a raid on French shipping on Lake Champlain. On their march to St Francis, the rangers sloshed for nine days through a bog in which they

Much of the Lake George region remains unchanged since Rogers' rangers campaigned throughout it. This is a view of the lake's island-clogged First Narrows as seen from the slopes of Black Mountain. (Author's photo)

Drawing based on a 1666 Iroquois pictograph showing: (left), a returning hunter with tumpline pack; (right), a prisoner holding a gourd rattle and bound with a tumpline at neck and arms. (Author's drawing)

43

When Rogers' expedition
marched through the swamps
east of Missisquoi Bay, en route
to St Francis, sleeping berths
were made by the rangers,
who "fell saplins, and laid them
across each other, in form of a
raft, and cover'd them over
with boughs and leaves."
(Author's drawing)

"could scarcely get a Dry Place to sleep on." Rogers himself is said to have escaped pursuing Indians after his March 1758 battle by sliding down a smooth mountain slope nearly 700ft (210m) long. His four-month mission to Detroit and back in 1760 covered over 1,600 miles (2,500km), one of the most remarkable expeditions in all American history.

At campaign's end, of course, there were rewards to be enjoyed. In late August 1758, Rogers gave his company "a barrell of Wine treat," and after a large bonfire was lit, the men "played round it" in celebration of recent British victories. As the Richelieu valley was being swept of French troops in 1760, provincial captain Samuel Jenks wrote with delight, "Our rangers … inform us the ladys are very kind in the neighbourhood, which seems we shall fare better when we git into the thick setled parts of the country." Natural wonders previously unseen by any British soldiers, including Niagara Falls, awaited the 200 rangers who followed Rogers that year to lay claim to Canada's Great Lakes country for England, and to win the friendship of some of the very tribes they had so often fought.

ESPRIT DE CORPS

With more than a little justification, Rogers' rangers considered themselves a breed apart from the redcoats and provincials, and they roundly resented outside attempts to disturb their special fraternity. But factors beyond the special forces nature of their service also bonded them. Many had been neighbors back on the frontier; chances are that our Derryfield farmer had hunted, trapped, or scouted alongside the Rogers brothers, John Stark, and other men of the corps. In December 1756, Robert Rogers admonished Loudoun that ranger recruits "expect to serve under such Officers only as they have a thorough knowledge of."

Discipline, mutiny, and desertion

Rogers himself, knowing both the temper and the abilities of his rangers, exerted a very cautious hand over them. Like most colonial forces, there were virtually no social divisions between Rogers and his men, and the major's generosity of bonhomie and money – not to mention his characteristic coolness under fire – made him a well liked and respected leader. One anecdote preserved in a town history typifies this sometimes informal relationship. While resting during their return from a scouting excursion, one ranger of the party still had rum left in his canteen, "to whom the Major offered a dollar for the rum. The soldier, suffering not less than his officer, replied, 'Major Rogers, I love you, but love myself better' – at the same moment turning up the canteen and swallowing the rum."

For the first two years of the war the rangers, despite their rough-hewn nature, had been involved in few serious infractions. Even the rate of ranger desertion was considerably lower than that of the regular army. But in December 1757, an incident marred this record. A small mob of rangers, incensed because two of their fellows had been jailed on the charge of stealing rum, chopped down the Rogers' Island whipping post. "If the Rangers are to be flogged," several were heard to declare, "there would be no more Rangers." An attempt to storm the guardhouse failed, and six of the men were arrested. Colonel William Haviland, commanding at Fort Edward, had the six "mutineers" thrown into the fort's jail. He also refused Rogers' request to have them sit before a ranger court of inquiry.

During Rogers' 1760 mission across the Great Lakes, he won the trust of the Ottawa war chief, Pontiac, who not only allowed the rangers to continue their journey to Fort Detroit but advised other tribes along the way to do so as well. (Author's drawing)

An in absentia inquiry was held anyway, and, because ranger testimony resulted in little more than a green wall of silence, "nothing final" could be decided as to the guilt or innocence of the accused. Rogers then advised Haviland that "most of his men will desert" unless he "put an end to this Affair." The colonel replied that if Rogers could catch one of the deserters, "I would endeavour to have him hanged as an example." Only the diplomatic intervention of General Abercromby salvaged the situation and put an end to Rogers' threat to resign. "Without him these four companies would be good for nothing," the general wrote to Loudoun. Despite the incident, Loudoun soon ordered Rogers to raise five more ranger companies.

Haviland's low opinion of ranger discipline ("a Riotous sort of people") had been exacerbated by Captain James Abercrombie of the 42nd, whose experience with a scouting party in November had left him appalled at what he deemed the ranger officers' failure to have "the best command of their men." When they uttered "the Indian hollow" to draw out an enemy party from Fort Carillon, "they yelled as if Hell had broken loose … I did every thing in my power to make them hold their tongues & behave as they ought to doe. I even knocked several of them down & damn'd their Officers for a set of Scoundrels." Abercrombie, who nine months earlier had praised Rogers' "conduct and your mens behaviour" after their winter battle, believed that only Rogers was capable of keeping them in line. In fact, Abercrombie was blind to the fact that his own highhandedness throughout the scout had aroused the rangers' contempt, making them loath to co-operate with him.

The connection between excessive restraints and increasing desertion was made plain in 1759 when General Amherst, ironically Rogers' constant friend among the redcoat elite, instituted a harsher discipline upon the army as a whole. Twenty-two rangers deserted from Moses Brewer's company in March. In April, 17 left the company of James Rogers, Robert's older brother. Five fled Jonathan Burbank's company in July. Nevertheless, at a strength of ten companies Rogers' corps was at its peak that year, and it shared in the triumphant capture of forts Carillon and St Frederic on Lake Champlain.

National and ethnic makeup

Most of Rogers' men were Scots-Irish or English. Others were Irish, Welsh, Dutch, German, Spanish, or Portuguese, representing several religions. Lieutenant "Billy" Philips was the product of an Indian mother and a father of Dutch or French ancestry. There were black rangers, some of them free men, others servants. Rogers' own servant, Prince, was black, and in 1762 was described as having "been several Years in the Service to the Westward." Three of the 1759 companies at Lake George were entirely composed of Native Americans.

Knapsacks of cowhide, or of "Deerskins dressed with the Hair on," were used by the rangers, regulars, and provincials. This one is based on knapsacks seen in paintings of redcoats by David Morier and Edward Penny. Left: a blanket-pack wrapped by a tumpline; often a bearskin or other rain-repellant cover was tied around it. (Author's drawing)

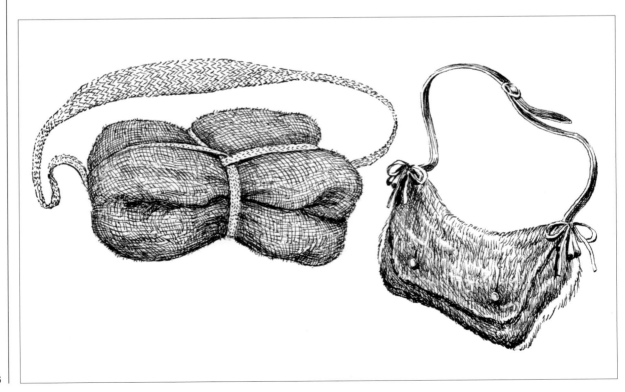

The ruins of Amherst's large fort at Crown Point, as they appear today. In 1773, the fort's powder magazine blew up, creating stone shells of the barracks. (Author's photo)

RANGERS IN BATTLE

Though an increasingly unfashionable word with some historians, there is no better one than "savage" to describe the nature of the forest combat the colonial rangers engaged in.

Scalps and prisoners

If such commanders as General Abercromby considered scalping "a barbarous Custom first introduced by the French, and of no use to the Cause," they rarely forbade their own partisans from practicing it against the Canadians and Indians. During lulls in Rogers' 1758 Battle on Snowshoes, the rangers broke from their positions and "begun to Sculp" the enemy dead around them (the price for hair had risen to £10). At Louisbourg that summer, according to one correspondent, "the Rangers and Highlanders are extremely Serviceable, daily bringing in Prisoners and Scalps."

Prisoners taken by the rangers could suffer immediate execution if the rangers found themselves ambushed. When a hidden enemy party opened fire on Rogers' marching column on 21 January 1757, the wounded Private Thomas Brown "retir'd into the Rear, to the Prisoner I had taken on the Lake, Knock'd him on the Head and killed him, lest he should Escape and give Information to the Enemy." During Wolfe's advance on Quebec, Captain Moses Hazen's ranger company had orders to "kill all, and give no quarter," according to Private David Perry. After a skirmish, a wounded French priest "begged earnestly for quarters: but the Captain told the men to kill him. Upon which, one of them deliberately blew his brains out."

Yet there were also moments of humanity and mercy, as when General Amherst in 1760 assured the weeping Canadian women and children of Isle Perrot that they would not be given over to the Iroquois.

"Everyone was melted into Compassion at the miserable Sight," noted a British officer, "even the very Rangers whose Hearts are none of the softest, seemed glad when they were ordered back without their Prisoners."

Close combat

Rangers had to be well trained in hand-to-hand fighting. In his Rule XIII, Rogers instructed that one's fire should be reserved until the enemy "approach very near." While the latter were absorbing the shock of your discharge, you should rush "upon them with your hatchets and cutlasses." Connecticut provincial ranger Thomas Knowlton shot an Indian crawling toward him during the battle near Fort Anne, and after reloading his musket ran forward to take the scalp. In the memoir penned by Knowlton's son, suddenly "10 or 12 Indians jumped up from the grass on all sides of him." Knowlton "shot down the nearest warrior, and … regained his comrades in safety, though pursued by a shower of balls." Later he encountered a burly Frenchman; both men aimed their pieces and pulled trigger, and both muskets misfired. In the ensuing struggle the Frenchman was gaining the advantage when another provincial arrived and took him prisoner.

At the 1757 winter battle, Thomas Brown ran for the cover of a large rock, but "there started up an Indian from the other Side; I threw myself backward into the Snow, and it being very deep, sunk so low that I broke my Snowshoes (I had Time to pull 'em off, but was obliged to let my Shoes go with them). One Indian threw his Tomahawk at me, and another was just upon seizing me; but I happily escaped and got to the Centre of our Men, and fix'd myself behind a large Pine."

Massachusetts ranger Hugh Maxwell found himself chased by Indians while on a scout near Ticonderoga. "I saw two Indians throw down their guns and pursue me with tomahawks." After a mile (1.6km), he paused to catch his breath, looked back, and saw one Indian 'within twenty feet [6m] of me and the other near by … I shot the first dead in his tracks." Resuming his run, Maxwell soon heard the second Indian stumble over a fallen hemlock tree "with a grunt, and there I left him."

The big battles

Rangers often fought in the great battles and sieges of the war. While General Wolfe launched his disastrous assault on the heights of Montmorency on 31 July 1759, "our company remained on the bank, with our muskets loaded, as a kind of corps de reserve," wrote ranger David Perry. "General Wolfe stood with us, where we could see the whole maneuver." At the beginning of Abercromby's attack on the French lines at Ticonderoga, Rogers' rangers drew first blood, driving in advanced enemy pickets. The battle developed into one of the most intense of Rogers' career, the musketballs coming "by hands full," in the words of future ranger Perry, then a provincial soldier. At sunset the rangers formed a rearguard to cover the retreat of the bloodied British Army.

During the failed French attempt to capture Fort William Henry in March 1757, John Stark's rangers in the besieged garrison "behavd with a great deal of Courage & would have rushed out against the Enemy," noted one officer, "but the Major [William Eyre] thought it prudent to keep them in the Fort." Spearheading the landing of Amherst's invasion boats at Cape Breton Island on 8 June 1758 were Captain James Rogers' ranger company and a small detachment of light infantry. "The Rangers landed first," noted a shipboard observer, under "Rocks [that] were extremely rough & hard to climb, being almost perpendicular." At their summit they engaged units of French soldiers and Micmac Indians long enough to enable Wolfe's main brigade to land and sweep the enemy inland. Brigadier Charles Lawrence later wrote that the New England rangers "behavd at Landing so as to do great Honor to themselves and the Country they came from."

At the beginning of the siege of Isle aux Noix in August 1760, Rogers' companies were among the first to land on the east shore of the Richelieu River, and later helped guide and drag artillery through the trees to establish a battery opposite the French naval force. Buccaneer-like, a party of his rangers, armed only with tomahawks, swam aboard one of the vessels and captured her.

During General James Murray's 1760 battle with General François de Levis outside Quebec, Hazen's rangers experienced heavy fighting on the left wing of the redcoat army. The French won the day, pushing Murray's force back into the city. Posted outside the walls at night, the rangers skirmished with enemy partisans and raided the French trenches, just as Rogers' men had done during the siege of Fort Carillon in 1759.

Some typical bush fights

Rogers gave those rangers he picked for his January 1757 scout two days to prepare at Fort William Henry, supplying them with "provisions, snowshoes, &c." But in most cases rangers had little time to get ready for a trek. When word arrived at the Lake George camp in August 1758 of an enemy force in the vicinity, provincial Abel Spicer and his fellow draftees were given less than an hour to get their kits together and jump into boats to join the pursuit party under Rogers and Putnam.

Spicer experienced bush fighting at its most intense ten days later when the detachment was ambushed by Marin's large raiding force. Stationed at the rear of the column, Rogers "wheeled to the right which brought us into a half circle and then we began to drive them," wrote Spicer. "Come up you French dogs, like men!" he heard Rogers shout. Another man observed the major shoot down a "Sachem 6 foot 4 Inches [1.93m] high proportionably made … the Largest Indian Ever Rogers saw." Added Spicer, "the fight lasted about two hours but after [the enemy] had gone off we buried the dead and brought off the wounded."

Many wounded rangers were not always so lucky. Thomas Brown was but one of several disabled rangers found by the Indians after the January 1757 battle. One warrior approached a badly wounded Captain Thomas Speakman, "and stripp'd and scalp'd him alive," before the eyes of the hidden Brown. After the Indian left, Speakman begged Brown, "For God's sake! To give him a Tomahawk, that he might put an End to his Life! I refus'd him, and Exhorted him as well as I could to pray for Mercy." After he died, Brown "pull'd off his Stockings … and put them on my own Legs."

Some engagements took place on the lake waters. In November 1755, Rogers commanded 30 men in four bateaux, each one armed with two pieces of light artillery. With three boats he pursued two large war canoes and attacked a small French fort near the northern end of Lake George. Two broadsides sent the garrison of 100 French regulars scurrying into the woods.

Five years later, at Pointe au Fer, near the northern end of Lake Champlain, Rogers' raiding party of 203 rangers and 12 British light infantry was engaged by over 300 French and Indians. "They began the attack on our left wing," noted one ranger officer, "with usual intrepidity and yelling, which was returned as briskly by our own men." Some of the heaviest fighting centered around the beached ranger boats. "When the Indians found that they could not load fast enough … they took up stones and threw stones at us, on which our men halloo'd to them, that they would likewise fight with stones, and give them an equal chance, which routed them from behind the boats."

While this seriocomic exchange was going on, Rogers had ordered a lieutenant with 70 rangers to circle through a bog and attack the enemy's rear. This surprise move ended the battle, the French and Indians "immediately" fleeing, taking 17 of their wounded with them and leaving behind 32 dead. Rogers' losses amounted to 17 dead and 11 wounded. "We got 34 fine guns," wrote the ranger officer. French deserters later revealed that after returning to Montreal, the Indians decided to go "home to a man, to do honour to their departed friends, not all the French could do being able to prevail upon them to stay."

THEIR LEGACY

Although it took the capture of the major Canadian forts and cities to finally seal the victory for Britain, the colonial rangers had been the point and flank men, paving the way through the vast belts of wilderness lying between the opposing empires. Rogers' corps had also helped to shorten the war by neutralizing the power of the enemy's partisans, defeating them at the La Chute River, Fort Anne, Wood Creek, St Francis, Pointe au Fer, and in dozens of smaller engagements. (His men suffered only one major defeat, the Battle on Snowshoes in 1758, and one technical draw, the winter fight of 1757.) By clearly demonstrating how useless machinelike linear tactics were in the shaggy northern forests, the rangers also inspired reforms in the regular army, including the creation of its first light infantry companies.

If the rangers in their own time had endured some harsh criticisms, especially from several unshakeably Old World generals, they nevertheless proved themselves a class of warrior whose overall record was one of unexpected achievement against daunting odds. Some of the rangers under Rogers' command – John Stark, Israel Putnam, Moses Hazen, Jonathan and David Brewer, Joseph Waite, Joseph Senter, David Gilman, and Thomas Knowlton – became generals or colonels in the American army of the Revolution. Others, like William Stark, Phineas Atherton, Stephen Holland, James Rogers, and Robert Rogers himself, became Loyalist officers.

Rogers' own contributions to this unique military art were so significant, in fact, that his rules for ranging are still being issued to United States Special Forces, and remain posted at Ranger battalion headquarters at Fort Benning, Georgia.

COLLECTIONS, MUSEUMS, AND RE-ENACTMENTS

Because almost none of the ranger companies of the northern colonies, even during the last, great conflict of 1755–60, seem to have worn uniforms that remained the same from year to year, ascribing a ranger lineage to any clothing artifact is almost impossible. Aside from those rare occasions when several ranger companies received the same uniform – for example, the rangers assigned to join Wolfe on his 1759 Quebec campaign – most of the time the men were dressed in whatever short, ready-to-wear clothing could be purchased by their captains in military or civilian stores, or in attire sewn by company tailors.

A mere handful of surviving accouterments can be verified as ranger in origin because their owners' names were engraved upon them: for instance, the 1756 powder horns of captains Robert Rogers and Jacob Cheeksaunkun. Even many relics unearthed on the site of the Rogers' Island hut camp cannot always be linked to the rangers because that site also saw occupation by provincial and regular troops. Buttons recently declared to have been worn by Rogers' own company, with back-to-back Rs as an insignia, are outright hoaxes inspired by an entry in an equally fraudulent ranger "diary," and the purchase of such "relics" and their reproductions should be avoided.

The displayed collection of the museum at the reconstructed Fort Ticonderoga, in Ticonderoga, New York (www.fort-ticonderoga.org/museum.htm), is one of the most extensive in terms of colonial military culture and artifacts. The above-mentioned powder horns can be seen there, as can Captain Thomas Davies' oil painting, *View of the Lines at Lake George*, 1759. Other accouterments and weapons of the kinds used by rangers – muskets, fusils, bayonets, pistols, tomahawks, knives, cartridge boxes, canteens, ice creepers, and so on – are also exhibited, in rich abundance. The museum collection housed at Fort William Henry, in Lake George Village, New York (www.fortwilliamhenry.com/fortmus.htm), is smaller-scale but equally fascinating, including such curios as an Indian dugout canoe found in the lake, small leather bullet pouches, and photographs of skeletons unearthed in a nearby soldiers' cemetery, some showing evidence of violent demises.

The tiny collection in the Crown Point Visitors Center, Crown Point, New York, contains a model of Amherst's gigantic fort, and an unusual, dark green-colored powder horn marked J. TUTE, indicating its possible ownership by ranger Captain James Tute. The Rogers' Island Visitors Center, in the Hudson River at Fort Edward, New York (www.rogersisland.org), exhibits a collection of military relics from the locality, from ceramics to belt buckles, coins to cuff links, arrowheads to buckshot. The new owner of much of the lower half of the island intends to erect a monument to the rangers and a second museum, containing freshly uncovered artifacts. Other collections can be found in such reconstructed forts as Old Fort Niagara, New York; Fort Number Four, New Hampshire; and Fort Ligonier, Pennsylvania.

Ranger living history units have been in existence since the 1950s. The oldest and largest group is Major John C. Jaeger's Michiganheadquartered ranger battalion (www.rogersrangers.com), which includes members in 20 states, Canada, and the United Kingdom. The Seven Year War Website (www.militaryheritage.com/7yrswar.htm) offers links to other ranger re-enactment companies. One unique unit, Harmon's Snowshoe Company (www.snowshoemen.com), recreates New England rangers from the late 17th century up to the last French and Indian war. Many ranger re-enactors attend the French and Indian War "Encampments" at Fort Ticonderoga (usually near the end of June), and at Crown Point (in August), where they set up their camps within the ruins of the big British fort and the smaller French one. Both events are open to the public.

GLOSSARY

Abatis	Defensive outerwork of felled trees, their branches toward the enemy and often sharpened.
Bark house	Shed-like shelter made of sheets of bark laid over a pole framework.
Bath rug	Heavy woolen material made in Bath, England, used for overcoats, cloaks, and bedgowns.
Battalion	Regimental subdivision, numbering anywhere from four to five companies.
Blockhouse	Two-storied defensive log building, its upper floor slightly overhanging the lower. Sometimes standing alone to guard roads, they were also built at the corners of frontier stockades.
Boom	Connected floating logs made to obstruct navigation.
Bounty	Monetary inducement for a recruit, often including an advance toward his purchase of arms and clothing.
Brevet	Honorific or temporary rank advancement given to an officer, enabling him to expand his command, especially in the field.
Cadre	The dependable veteran nucleus of a military unit, especially officers.
Chitterlings	Frilling down the front of a shirt.
Cordwood	Cut wood neatly stacked in piles.
Corps	A body of troops, sometimes representing a variety of units, unified for service under one commander.
Corps de reserve	Troops held back from the battle line until needed.
Countersign	A password.
Draughts	Checkers.
Furlough	Leave of absence granted to a soldier.
Garrison	A fort or a stockade (also the troops residing in it); a strongly built dwelling designed to withstand an attack.
Glacis	The sloping outer side of a fort's ditch.
Independent company	A company independently raised and not associated with a regiment.
Indian stocking	A legging of wool or leather, designed to protect the leg against snake bites, insects, and thorns.
Jockey cap	In its simplest form, a cap of felt or leather with a visor.
Log	A verb meaning to create a defensive work by arranging fallen tree trunks into a rough breastwork.
Partisan	An irregular; an unconventional warrior; a ranger.
Platoon firing	Volley-firing by a sub-unit of aligned soldiers.
Portage	To carry a canoe or boat overland between streams, rivers, or lakes.
Provincials	Troops raised in the American colonies.
Regiment	A body of troops composed of one or more battalions, commanded by a colonel. Regiments from Britain were

	numbered. In America, they were identified by colony.
Serge	A twilled, durable woolen cloth, used for jackets, coats, and linings.
Shot bag	Leather or linen bag holding ball and smaller shot; a bullet pouch.
Street firing	The front ranks in a marching column firing by turns, those with already discharged muskets retiring on either side of the column to reform and reload at its end.
Stroud	Woolen blanket or coating material, often with a white or colored border, much favored by Indians.
Surtout	A short greatcoat or watchcoat.

BIBLIOGRAPHY

Amherst, Jeffery, *The Journal of Jeffery Amherst*, The Ryerson Press, Toronto and Chicago, 1931

Bellico, Russell P., *Chronicles of Lake George: Journeys in War and Peace*, Fleischmanns, New York, 1995

Bougainville, Louis Antoine de, *Adventure in the Wilderness*, Journals, 1756–1760, Norman, Oklahoma, 1964

Cuneo, John R., *Robert Rogers of the Rangers*, Oxford University Press, New York, 1959

Grant, Anne, *Memoirs of an American Lady, Vol. II*, London, 1808

Knox, Captain John, *The Siege of Quebec and the Campaign in North America, 1757–1760*, ed. Brian Connell, The Folio Society, London, 1976

Loescher, Burt Garfield, *The History of Rogers' Rangers*, three volumes, published in California, 1947, 1957, 1969; reprinted in 2000–02 by Heritage Books of Maryland

O'Callaghan, E. B., ed., *Documents Relating to the Colonial History of the State of New York*, Weed, Parsons & Co., Albany, 1858

Pargellis, Stanley, ed., *Lord Loudoun in North America*, Archon Books, New York, 1968

Pargellis, Stanley, ed., *Military Affairs in North America*, Archon Books, Hartford, 1969

Perry, Captain David, *Recollections of an Old Soldier*, Windsor, Vermont, 1822

Pouchot, Captain Pierre, *Memoirs of the Late War in North America*, Old Fort Niagara Association, Inc., Youngstown, 1994

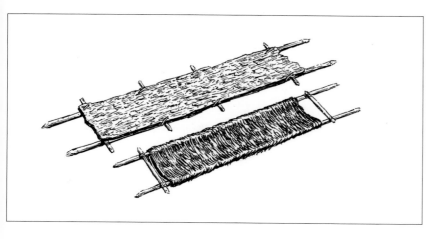

Litters for carrying wounded men were sometimes made by attaching strong sheets of bark to two poles, or by wrapping animal skins or blankets around them. (Author's drawing)

53

Rogers, Major Robert, *A Concise Account of North America*, John Millan, London, 1765

Rogers, Major Robert, *The Annotated and Illustrated Journals of Major Robert Rogers*, annotations by Timothy J. Todish, illustrations and captions by Gary S. Zaboly, Fleischmanns, New York, 2002

Smith, James, "An Account of the Remarkable Occurrences in the Life and Travels of Colonel James Smith," in Archibald Loudoun, ed., *A Selection of Some of the Most Interesting Narratives of Outrages, Committed by the Indians in Their Wars with the White People*, Vol. II, A. Loudon, Carlisle, Pennsylvania, 1808

Stark, Caleb, *Memoir and Official Correspondence of General John Stark*, Boston, 1972; reprint: Heritage Books, Maryland, 1999

Near Ticonderoga in March 1759 Rogers and 90 rangers and Indians captured seven French soldiers and beat back three attacks by over 200 of the enemy, in weather "so severe it is almost impossible to describe it," he wrote. "They could not stand against our Marksmen." He was able to carry his prisoners away "without any opposition the Enemy being affraide to pursue us any Further." (Author's drawing)

COLOR PLATES

A: PRIVATE, CAPTAIN JOHN LOVEWELL'S NEW ENGLAND RANGER COMPANY, 1725

A successful 1724 raid by New Englanders on Norridgewock, a village of the Eastern Abenaki located on Maine's Kennebec River 60 miles (100km) from its Atlantic mouth, showed other colonials that war could be taken to the Indians' own home base. Such deep penetrations into enemy country required a breed of soldiers willing not only to track and fight like Native Americans, but also to dress, arm, and equip themselves somewhat in their manner. Captain John Lovewell's volunteer ranger company of 1724–25, recruited mainly in frontier towns of Massachusetts and New Hampshire, largely met these unorthodox criteria. At the Battle of Lovewell's Pond on 9 May 1725, the rangers' backgrounds as sharpshooting woodsmen enabled them to fight to a draw a Pigwacket war party that outnumbered their own by more than two to one.

1. This private exemplifies the hybrid European/Indian composition of Lovewell's men. His knitted cap, buckskin breeches, shirt, and short jacket are typical of white farmers

The vicious nature of forest warfare was often toned down in reports designed for public consumption. In his published Journals, Robert Rogers refrained from admitting that he and his men had engaged in collecting scalps for bounty money, as they had during the 1758 Battle on Snowshoes. (Author's drawing)

and workmen of the day; but his leather leggings, moccasins, beaded tumpline, and bearskin-wrapped blanket pack are Indian innovations sensibly designed for easier traveling in the forest. He also carries a small hatchet, or tomahawk, in a rough leather case, and his musket is protected from the elements by a guncase of deer or moose skin. Buckshot and ball are carried in a small bag hanging before him, and a brass powder flask is held on a long rope, much like the one seen in L. Knyff's 1700 portrait of Lord Irwin in his hunting outfit. A "calabash" (gourd) contains water or rum, or a mixture of both.

2. Essentially non-uniformed civilians, Lovewell's rangers wore a variety of headgear. This style of cap, often seen in 18th-century depictions of European hunters and trappers, has a back flap that can be lowered in bad weather and buttoned under the chin to protect the ears and neck.

3. A bearskin fur cap based on a pattern common in England and the Continent.

4. Another European-style cap with a back flap, this one lined with fur. The visor could be lifted up, or worn down as shown. Such caps can be seen in Carle Van Loo's painting, The Bear Hunt. Native Americans made winter hoods of a similar design, though without visors, from the pelts of beaver, moose, deer, and other animals.

5. A powder horn of 1720s New England, its shape based on an actual relic said to have been owned by Paugus, who led the Pigwackets at Lovewell's Pond. Paugus' horn measures over 13in (33cm) in length and has crude carvings of deer, snakes, grouse, and two turtles, the totem of the tribe.

6. A sack made of strong linen, of an old pattern resembling a modern duffel bag. This and other "snapsacks" of similar design were carried by both military men and civilians (such as traveling tinkers) of the 17th and 18th centuries.

7. An Indian toboggan, varying in length from 6 to 12ft (1.8–3.7m), usually made of two planks of green spruce, birch, or elm wood that were lashed together with rawhide. The front of the sled was rolled back and held with guy ropes to the main body. Rawhide lines or ropes drew the toboggan, which could haul supplies and other heavy loads over deep snow. Sometimes a tumpline was used to draw it; on occasion dogs were employed, much like huskies.

8. Belt dagger made by a colonial blacksmith, 12in (30cm) in length, with a grip of cherry wood.

9. Dogs were integral to New England hunters, and they accompanied Lovewell's men into the central New Hampshire wilderness to sniff out enemy Indians. On one occasion the rangers muzzled them as they approached a sleeping party of Abenakis. After opening fire on the Indians, the men took the muzzles off the dogs, who then brought down fleeing survivors.

10. A long sporting flintlock musket dating from the period of Queen Anne's War (1702–14), with a typically flat lock plate and stock of fruit wood. This specimen was manufactured by John Cookson, a Boston gunsmith.

11. A flintlock of the late 17th century called a "doglock," for the dog, or catch, holding the rear of the cock. This particular relic was owned by Captain Samuel Gorton, a veteran of King William's War (1690–97), who died in 1724.

12. One of the incentives for Lovewell's "Indian hunters" was the bounty of £100 per Indian scalp offered by the Boston General Court. On one raid in January 1725, Lovewell's men harvested ten scalps, and brought them back Indian-style, each one stretched on a small hoop made from a branch that was strung from the end of a pole, for a barbaric procession through the streets of Boston. Sometimes the skin-side of the trophy was painted.

B: RECRUITMENT AND TRAINING: FIRING AT MARKS, FORT WILLIAM HENRY, 1756

Excellent marksmanship, aside from scoutcraft and daring, is what made the best rangers. Former hunters and trappers most of them, they understood how a single well-aimed shot might alter the course of a skirmish or battle in the forest. Robert Rogers instructed his companies to practice firing at marks so frequently that at least one British commander, Lieutenant-colonel William Haviland, scolded him, considering it an "extravagance in Ammunition." But the training paid off; in their numerous engagements with their partisan enemies, the rangers inflicted so many casualties that on at least four occasions parties of French-allied Indians abandoned the campaign to return to their villages to treat their wounded and mourn their dead.

The scene depicts an informal session of target practice on a late summer's day in 1756, just outside Fort William Henry at the southern end of Lake George. "Shooting boards," according to the 1759 orderly book of the 42nd Highland Regiment, were "covered with paper and a black spot made in the middle." For those rangers – such as the green-clad man of Captain Humphrey Hobbs' independent company shown here – who were equipped with smoothbore muskets instead of more accurate rifled carbines, constant training in marksmanship was imperative. Both Hobbs' company and that of Captain Thomas Speakman had been raised that year largely in and around Boston; consequently many of the men were city dwellers and sailors, which made their strenuous training regimen all the more critical.

Both companies had arrived on the war front well dressed, each man in "a good Hunting Coat, Vest & Breeches, a pair of Indian Stockings [and] Shoes." The coats were probably much like hunting garments worn by gentlemen in the British Isles and Continental Europe, and were either green or brown for concealment purposes. Chest pockets carried spare flints and loose balls. Their headgear is unknown, but leather jockey caps were favored by many ranger units from Nova Scotia to South Carolina, and were sold in great quantities in the big cities. Instead of bullet pouches and powder horns, Hobbs' and Speakman's companies were issued cartridge boxes on straps.

"Shooting at marks," noted Rogers, was "a diversion much in use among the savages." Here, an officer of the Stockbridge Indian ranger company charges his piece for another shot. His finely laced and ruffled shirt, stained with drops of vermilion face paint, has seen better days. A Mohawk war captain sits nearby, the lock of his gun protected by a bearskin case. The details of his fine blue stroud matchcoat, decorated straps, wampum jewelry, moccasins, and feathers are culled from the portrait of John Johnson and a Mohawk emissary attributed to Benjamin West in the mid-1760s.

In the center of the group, a ranger of one of the provincial regiments shoots at a target. His attire is not unlike that worn in the field by part-time ranger Rufus Putnam of Massachusetts: "nothing but a shirt and Indian Stockings."

At far left stands a "bush loper," a Mohawk Valley or Albany Dutchman transformed into a pseudo-Indian. Many such men were employees in the Indian trade, and very familiar with Iroquois customs and methods of scouting and fighting. Some even shaved their heads down to scalplocks. This man carries his buck and ball in a fringed Mohawk-style bullet bag.

In 1758, the ten best marksmen of each redcoat regiment under General James Abercromby were equipped with "Riffled Barrell Guns," and detached into a company of ranger-like troops for the expedition against French-held Fort Carillon at the northern end of Lake George.

C: RANGERS' KIT, EQUIPMENT, WEAPONS, AND SPECIAL CLOTHING

To be effective as warriors in the unforgiving American wilderness, rangers had to abandon the spit and polish regimens of British regular troops and develop their own set of rules regarding weapons, equipment, and clothing. In time, the redcoats themselves were forced to adopt many ranger methods and items, a revolutionary move that enabled them to better operate in the forest under motley and daunting conditions of weather and terrain.

1. A c.1735–50, .75 caliber "Long Land Pattern" Brown Bess musket, sawed down from its overall length of $61\frac{3}{4}$ in (157cm) to a lighter, more maneuverable $50\frac{3}{8}$ in (128cm), with its sight repositioned. Excavations on Rogers' Island have unearthed cut ends of musket barrels ranging from 4 to 8in (10–20cm) in length. Often the wooden stocks themselves were "dressed." To kill the glint of sunlight on metal parts, the stocks were stained brown, blue, or black. Early models of the Brown Bess had wooden ramrods. A small leather "hammercap," or "hammer slat," kept the lock's frizzen safe from an accidental fall of the flint-laden cock. Although some of them undoubtedly used Besses, Rogers' rangers were encouraged to bring their own weapons from home, or else to purchase guns generally lighter than those issued to the regulars. As New

A rare eyewitness glimpse of a French and Indian War army on the move: Captain Thomas Davies' 1760 watercolor of Amherst's troops advancing toward Montreal down the La Chine rapids of the St Lawrence River. Two companies of rangers (Waite's and Ogden's) accompanied the expedition, in whaleboats. The canoe-borne Indians are some of Sir William Johnson's Iroquois. The descent cost Amherst 84 drowned men. (Thomas Davies, National Archives of Canada/C-000577)

Hampshire's Governor Benning Wentworth recommended in 1759, the colony's recruits should "find themselves Arms … as the King's Arms are very heavy."

2. An English-made, .65 caliber carbine with a rifled barrel, $57\frac{1}{2}$in (146cm) long, with its socket bayonet. By early 1758, Rogers' rangers, according to a captain of the 27th Regiment of Foot, were armed "mostly with riffled Barrels." These were probably much like the "300 Riffled carbines … with Bayonets [and] Iron Rammers" originally ordered for Colonel George Prevost's 60th Regiment (the Royal Americans) in early 1757. (Because they had iron rammers and bayonets they were definitely not German-made Jaeger rifles, as some have theorized.) No existing specimen is known to the artist/author; however, the type shown here is illustrated after the smooth-bored "Light Infantry Carbine" introduced c.1757. The latter model, in fact, became the main arm of General Thomas Gage's 80th Light Armed Regiment of Foot in 1759, and the weapon of the light companies of the other regular regiments under General Amherst that year.

3. Field officer's fusil, a short, streamlined musket generally weighing several pounds less than a Brown Bess. The specimen shown here was about $54\frac{1}{2}$in (138.5cm) long.

Ranger compasses. Upper left: "a Gold Ring … Containing in it a small Compass," advertised as lost by Captain John Gorham in a 1748 Boston newspaper (drawing is hypothetical). Upper right: pocket brass sundial compass found in an excavated hut on Rogers' Island (cap not shown). Bottom: according to Captain John Knox in 1757, Rogers' officers "usually carry a small compass fixed in the bottoms of their powder horns, by which to direct them, when they happen to lose themselves in the woods." (Author's drawing)

Fusils were often ornamented and engraved; some were mounted with silver furniture. Others had brass barrels. Calibers ranged from .60 to .73. Robert Rogers, John Stark, and Israel Putnam were all recorded as having carried "fuzees" into battle.

4. Belt hatchet or tomahawk, the steel blade under 6in (15cm) in length, from a specimen found at Fort William Henry. The I SPEAK imprint echoes similar mottos engraved into powder horns of the day, such as A HERO LIKE I CONQUER ALL. Sometimes called a "scalping ax," it served the dual purpose of dispatching enemies in close-quarter fighting and cutting one's way through thickets. Tomahawk blades of other sizes and shapes have been found at ranger campsites, but they are commonly 5–6in (13–15cm) long.

5. A pair of silver-mounted Queen Anne style screw-barrel (or "cannon-barrel") pistols, favorites of many officers and civilians. They could be carried in waist belts, greatcoat pockets, or saddle holsters. Loading was done through the breech of the unscrewed barrel, eliminating the need for a ramrod.

6. An American-made cutlass with a cylindrical wooden grip and iron hilt, its blade $26\frac{1}{2}$in (67cm) long. Cutlasses were often substitutes for belt hatchets. Ranger officers not on field service generally wore swords of a finer make, usually with silver hilts.

7. Folding clasp knives such as this bone-handled, brass-ended one were favored by rangers over sheath knives, and for obvious reasons were dubbed "scalping knives." Excavated relics have blades averaging 6in (15cm) in length. After being taken captive by French and Indians in March 1758, ranger lieutenant "Billy" Phillips managed to get "one hand loose, took a knife from his pocket, which he opened with his teeth, cut the strings that bound him, and escaped."

8. Small "spying-glasses," or "prospective glasses," often closing to only 4in (10cm) in length (such as this all-brass type), were carried by Rogers and his officers on scouts.

9. Rangers preferred shooting with loose ball and powder horn rather than with fixed cartridges. At Halifax in 1757, British captain John Knox observed that Rogers' men carried their ammunition in "a leathern, or seal's skin bag, buckled round their waist, which hangs down before." Belted bullet pouches were favored by New England hunters. A few rangers may have carried long leather shot pouches with spring chargers, or simple leather or canvas bullet pouches on shoulder straps.

10. A typical ranger round, as noted by Captain Knox, consisting of "a smaller shot, of the size of full-grown peas: six or seven of which, with a ball, they generally load." The French and Indian partisans also loaded their longarms, by one report, "with a ball and six swan shot."

11. An iron ice creeper, worn under the instep and held in place by thongs or buckled straps. Some creepers found on Rogers' Island are marked with the British broad arrow on their undersides.

12. A type of ice skate common to the 18th century, with straps, small iron peg for the heel of the thick moccasin or shoe, and three smaller points for the sole. Rogers sometimes sent skating parties scouting ahead of his main detachments. The enemy was also adept on skates: "the Canadians skate in the manner of the Dutch, exceedingly fast," noted Thomas Anburey in the 1780s, "but the Indians dart along like lightning."

13. Detail of a decorated leather legging, or "Indian stocking," as seen in Benjamin West's 1770 painting, *The Death of General Wolfe*. A beaded leather strap connects the legging to a waist belt (unseen). Two black garters, tipped

Copley's portrait of the colonial-born Captain George Scott, who commanded the British light infantry and ranger companies at Louisbourg in 1758, and the six ranger companies at Quebec the following year. He wears a cut-down uniform coat of his regiment (the 40th), and holds a leather jockey cap, typical ranger headgear. Note the waist cartridge box with attached powder horn, and short bayonet on his fusil. (Courtesy the Frick Art Reference Library)

with tinkling cones that sport red-dyed animal hair, hang from the point where the strap is attached to the legging. Selvages flap loosely along the side of the leg, and a garter of wampum, held in place with a fancy red tie, is strapped under the knee. Leather leggings, however, were not as common among the rangers as were those made of such coarse woolen materials as frieze, stroud, or rateen, generally green in color, as in (14), or dark blue. A ribbon or binding trims the edges of the cloth, and straps for belt and feet keep the legging from sagging.

15. A snowshoe of a shape common to the 18th-century New England frontier. Hide strings, and sinew of deer, moose or horse, made the netting. The front of the foot was

held to the snowshoe by a loop, while two long thongs, lashed around the heel, enabled the latter to be raised freely at every step.

16. A typically wide-brimmed, civilian Scotch bonnet, most often blue, although some colonial merchants sold them in "various colours." Military bonnets were also available (one New York store in 1763 sold surplus Highland uniforms, including "Private Mens Bonnets" and "Sergeants Bonnets"). Many rangers favored bonnets when going afield, perhaps because they were the sons and grandsons of Lowland Scots who had emigrated to Northern Ireland.

17. A simply made leather jockey cap, its upturned visor left unfaced. Noted one British officer, "Leather Caps … are much more convenient, & less troublesome than Hats, in our Excursions thro' the Woods, & by water." Another remarked how it was also "better adapted to the Hood of the Cloke than a Hatt."

18. Mitten made of blanket material. Others were made of knitted wool, or of beaver or other skins. One army contractor at Albany requested from a supplier in 1758 "100 prs. Mens Neatest Buck & Doe Skin Gloves," most likely for officers.

19. A hat with its brim cut down to within 2–2$\frac{1}{2}$ in (5–6.5cm) of the crown to enable the ranger or soldier to move more easily through the woods. This was an innovation ordered for all of the troops, regular and provincial, under General Abercromby during the 1758 campaign against Fort Carillon.

20. A pair of "Snow Moggisons," as they were called in a list of clothing for a planned winter drive against Crown Point in 1756. Also termed "snow boots" or "shoe packs," these nearly waterproof items were made of moose or cowhide, and sometimes deerskin. Extra warmth was provided by liners made of blanket wool (as shown here), or of fur.

D: TACTICS AND COMBAT TECHNIQUES: RANGER DEFENSE PERIMETER, LA BARBUE CREEK, 1757

The clandestine nature of partisan warfare meant that ambush was the usual way for engagements to begin in the forest, with those laying the ambush generally becoming the victors. But on more than one occasion Robert Rogers was able to turn an enemy ambush into a ranger victory, or at least to inflict more casualties on the French and Indians than his own men suffered. The action on one of the branches of La Barbue Creek (today's Putnam's Creek), about 2 miles (3km) northwest of Ticonderoga, on 21 January 1757 was a textbook example of how a ranger detachment, after being lured into a deadly trap, could turn the tables on a superior enemy force.

"They fit them with their Walpeasses & with Blonder Boses," wrote a provincial diarist at Fort William Henry of Rogers' action against the French on Lake George in November 1755. Top: bronze wallpiece with swivel bar for mounting on a bow or gunnel, on display at Fort William Henry. Bottom: blunderbuss with swivel yoke. The funnel mouths of both guns allowed for fast loading during action, and fired either small shot or a one- or two-pound ball. (Author's drawing)

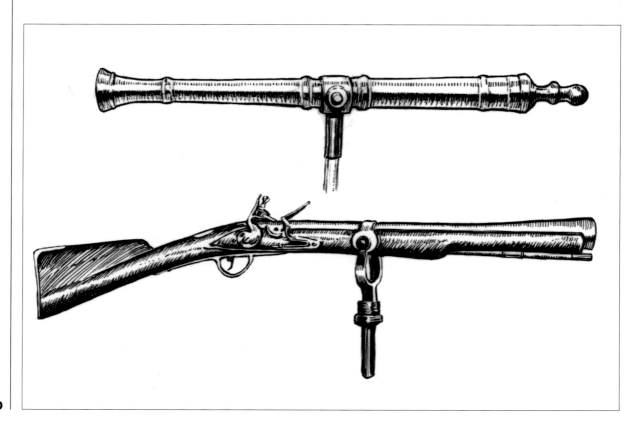

The day had begun, in fact, with Rogers' own ambush of a French provision-sleigh train on frozen Lake Champlain, midway between forts Carillon (at Ticonderoga), and St Frederic (Crown Point). With seven prisoners in tow, he and his 74 rangers began the long march back to Fort William Henry. In mid-afternoon, while crossing the steep valley of a small rivulet, Rogers' single-file detachment was ambushed by a party of 120 French and Indians hidden on the crest of the far slope. Leading the advanced guard, Rogers was grazed in the head by a bullet. After being momentarily stunned, he managed to get his men quickly retreating back up the small hill they had just descended. Meanwhile, Lieutenant John Stark, with the main body, organized a stand atop the hill in a convenient grove of large pines.

Rogers' training had paid off: enemy pursuers, in the face of a constant fire from Stark's position, fell back. On his rejoining Stark, Rogers ordered the lieutenant to stay where he was as the center of the ranger line, and posted himself with a party on the right flank. Ensign Jonathan Brewer commanded another party on the left, and Robert's older brother Ensign James Rogers, with about a dozen men, stayed in the rear to act as a reserve. All told, Rogers had but 57 rangers left after the initial ambush to hold off an enemy force that now outnumbered his own by two to one. Nevertheless, as ranger private Thomas Brown noted, "the Engagement held, as near as I could guess, 5½ Hours, and … we killed more of the Enemy than we were in Number." Brown was only slightly exaggerating the number of French and Indian casualties; in fact, several other accounts agree that ranger marksmanship and tactics had killed at least 28 of the enemy on the spot and wounded over 30 more, with most of the latter dying of their wounds. Rogers' own detachment lost 13 dead and 14 wounded, despite the fact that it had been the victim of ambush.

The illustration depicts the ranger lines at the height of the battle. In the right foreground is one end of Brewer's left flank party; in the left foreground is Stark's center; in the left background, Rogers' right flank wards off an attempted enemy encirclement of the hill. In the middle background, the ranger reserve party awaits its orders to rush to any threatened point.

The Indian tactic of two men defending a tree, with one of them firing while the other reloads, had been sensibly adopted by many white frontier soldiers. One of the foreground rangers spits a musket ball into the barrel of his musket, which speeded up the loading process (as much as six to eight bullets could be held in the mouth).

In this battle, the French and Indians never got close enough to the rangers' perimeter for hand-to-hand combat, the affair having settled down to a lethal sniping contest, the adversaries "yelling and making all the Noise they could." When dusk fell, Rogers ordered his men to hold their fire and not to speak. This drew the curious enemy forward, who walked into a deadly ranger volley and were driven back with more losses.

A ranger officers' council of war analyzed their situation. Their supply of ammunition was "almost expended," and they knew that French and Indian reinforcements would arrive in the morning to overwhelm them. It was decided to abandon the field and carry off their wounded. Somehow that freezing night, the 54 survivors managed to make a wide detour around the enemy positions and arrive at Lake George at 8am. A few badly wounded rangers, however, had been overlooked during the escape from the hill, and were captured by the French and Indians (including Thomas Brown, and one man with 11 bullets in his body, who died three weeks later).

Rogers' stand was all the more remarkable when one considers that many of his men were privates from the companies of captains Hobbs and Speakman, rangers mostly recruited along the Massachusetts coast just a half-year earlier. But the leadership of Rogers and his officers, coupled with hard training, is what made the difference. That, and the threat John Stark made to these neophytes to shoot "the first man who fled" during the battle.

E: DAILY LIFE: ROGERS' ISLAND, SPRING 1758

Beginning in the late summer of 1756, Major Robert Rogers' ranger companies were ordered to move south from Fort William Henry and encamp on a large island in the Hudson River just opposite Fort Edward. This position enabled scouts to fan out toward the lower reaches of Lake Champlain in the northeast, to Lake George in the north, to feeder streams of the Hudson in the northwest, and to Saratoga and Albany in the south. For three years the island would be Rogers' headquarters (and would be named after him), as well as the location of the barracks of most of his companies.

Those barracks consisted of rows of log huts, each hut averaging 11ft (3.4m) square in size. Archaeology on Rogers' Island, and eyewitness watercolors of the British camp at Crown Point in 1759 by Captain Thomas Davies of the Royal Artillery, confirm that these huts were built along company streets, each hut sharing a common wall with its neighbor. Roofs were made of boards or bark shingles, and chimneys were usually built of mortared stone; fireplaces were either of stone or brick. Chinking came from riverbank clay.

Rangers shunned living in tents; if no log hut was available, they would erect a "half-faced" shelter of bark or brush (much like a modern lean-to). One of their non-scouting duties was to go out to shoot bear, deer, and smaller game to supplement both their own larder and that of the redcoats. Animal hides were cleaned and dried: bearskins made excellent mattresses and rugs, deerskins were cut into moccasins, leggings, gun cases, and snowshoe netting.

The illustration depicts a day in May 1758, a month and a half before General Abercromby's grand push against Ticonderoga. In the left foreground, a ranger begins to repair his moccasin, punching holes into it with a steel awl. Instead of breeches, he wears ozenbrig linen trousers. Two ranger hunters return from a morning spent in the hills along the river's west bank. The rearmost hunter wears a checked shirt "painted" with a mixture of green and linseed oil that both served as camouflage and made the garment impervious to rain. The man in front wears a jacket made of "low priced green Cloths," and a black Scotch bonnet. Returning with the hunters is a wolf-dog. One of the latter breed was owned by Captain William Stark and called "Sergeant Beaubier," or "Boo-bear" for short.

In the right foreground, a ranger officer, just back to the island from a ride to Albany, reads aloud the news from other fronts in the latest issue of *The New-York Mercury* or *The*

Boston Gazette. His hat is laced with silver, and his surtout coat is made of green Bath rug (a heavy woolen material also used for cloaks, nightgowns, and bed coverlets). Listening to him is an officer of the 42nd Highlanders, one of many regulars who volunteered to learn ranger tactics in order to train their own regiments in wilderness operations. Instead of a customary kilt, the Highlander wears short trousers, which his checkered hose overlaps, and instead of shoes he wears moccasins. In the field he would also don Indian-style leggings (and his laced scarlet waistcoat would be left behind in camp). He drinks from a cup made from an ox horn. Seated next to him and taking a whiff of snuff is a ranger sergeant, his jacket laced and looped with silver.

In the hut at left, which has a deerskin for a temporary door, a ranger private plays cards under a grease lamp while smoking a short clay pipe. Atop the adjacent hut another ranger hammers fresh boards to its roof. In the background a frock-garbed ranger sweeps the paths around officers' huts. Near the river in the middle background is a "necessary house." In the far background Fort Edward sits on the Hudson's eastern shore, and beyond it stands a blockhouse guarding nearby roads.

F: COMBAT: THE ATTACK ON ST FRANCIS

Rogers' 4 October 1759 raid on the Abenaki mission village of St Francis, located just 3 miles (5km) south of the St Lawrence River, was the most daring coup of his entire career as a ranger leader. Yet his force of 142 men (whittled down from its original 200 due to sickness and lameness) was not wholly composed of green-clad rangers. There were small contingents of Stockbridge and Mohegan Indians, and white volunteers drawn from the ranks of ten provincial and regular regiments. It is to Rogers' credit as a commander that he was able to guide this disparate force so deep into French and Indian territory, and then succeed in carrying out General Amherst's order to destroy the Abenaki village.

The surprise attack was carried out by three divisions closing in on the riverside town from the south, east, and north. Operating in pairs, the men burst into the sleeping houses and killed what warriors they could find. They then set the church and houses on fire. A number of the Indians had hidden themselves in attics, where they perished in the flames. Others were killed or captured trying to flee across the river in canoes. Some 40 Abenakis died, which mirrored the percentage of casualties inflicted during French and Indian raids on Schenectady and Deerfield earlier in the century. Rogers lost only one Stockbridge ranger killed.

In the right foreground of the illustration, Major Rogers shouts orders to a New England provincial soldier who is escorting a freed white captive (a German girl seized by the Abenakis during a Mohawk River raid). Next to her are two of several Indian children Rogers would bring back to Crown Point. Behind them is a private of Gage's Light Infantry (the 80th Regiment). Elsewhere, rangers and other men of the detachment mop up the last resistance in the village.

St Francis surprised Rogers and his men in that it resembled a French town more than it did an Indian village. There was loot aplenty, too, especially from the Jesuit church: silver statues and candlesticks, bags of coins, rich belts of wampum, brooches, and so on. Grim reminders of Abenaki raids on frontier settlements hung on poles above

An iron swivel gun, also sometimes mounted on bateaux and whaleboats. (Collection of the Fort Ticonderoga Museum)

many of the lodge doors: "about 600 scalps, mostly English," in Rogers' own words.

G: AFTER THE BATTLE NEAR OLD FORT ANNE, AUGUST 1758

Rogers' battle with Captain Joseph Marin's force of French and Indians on 8 August 1758 was yet another example of his superb field leadership of a mixed detachment of rangers, provincials, and regulars (both light infantry and line troops). What began as an ambush of his column in the worst possible country for fighting – a thicket of second-growth saplings and low, often thorny, brush surrounding the site of old, abandoned Fort Anne – Rogers managed to turn into a victory by launching a heavy attack on Marin's left flank. When finally driven from the field, the enemy had left behind at least 54 dead, among them 15 Indians. Rogers' detachment had suffered 37 killed and about 40 wounded.

In the left foreground of the illustration a ranger scalps a Caughnawaga warrior, the latter's body "painted" almost entirely with charcoal. The black ranger in the center has already taken a French scalp and is threatening to remove the hair of a captured Marine private. (This figure's "green Jacket lined with red, Buckskin Breeches, blue Indian stockings, fine white Shirt, with Chitterlings, [and] spotted Silk Handkerchief," come from a newspaper description of a freed slave named Jacob, a Rogers' ranger veteran of the 1758 assault on Fort Carillon. Brought to the colonies from Africa, Jacob also bore tribal scars on each cheek.)

Most of the wounds suffered by Rogers' men were not serious, although one miraculously surviving Connecticut lieutenant had been shot eight times, "chopped with a tomahawk," and scalped. The usual method of carrying the non-walking wounded was to construct a litter made of two poles to which either a blanket or strong sheets of bark had been attached, Indian-fashion.

Another Indian conveyance was to carry the ailing man piggy-back by having him sit on a pack or blanket tied with a tumpline, the wide part of the line lying across the carrier's forehead. According to French captain Francois Pouchot, the Iroquois were known to carry their wounded in this manner "hundreds of leagues if they have no canoes." During the retreat from St Francis in 1759, Robert Rogers often carried the wounded Captain Amos Ogden "on his Back," especially when rivers had to be crossed.

A few of Marin's Indians returned to the battlefield and followed Rogers' detachment as it marched back to Fort Edward. Significantly, that night the Indians "found the English drinking and singing" around their campfires on the trail.

H: FRONTIER RANGERS, PONTIAC'S WAR, 1763–64

As the colonial frontier pushed deeper into the wilderness, white men engaged in warfare with the resisting Indians began to resemble their enemies more and more, mainly because time-tested Native American techniques, tools, and articles of clothing generally offered the most sensible means for dealing with the special conditions found in the forest.

1. Captain James Smith's ranger company, raised in 1763 to defend Pennsylvania's Conococheague valley against Pontiac-allied war parties, perfectly exemplified this growing willingness to meet the Indians on their own terms. A former captive of the Caughnawaga, Smith taught his rangers "the Indian discipline … which would answer the purpose much better than British." He also dressed them "uniformly in the Indian manner, with breech-clouts, leggins, mockasons, and green shrouds … In place of hats we wore red handkerchiefs, and painted our faces red and black, like Indian warriors." (Fourteen years later another Pennsylvania ranger named George Roush similarly painted his own face red, "with three black stripes across his cheeks, which was a signification of war.") The man depicted in the illustration holds a Pennsylvania-made, maple-stocked long rifle with a wooden patchbox. Among his accouterments is a wooden loading block holding ready-made, patched rifle balls. His moccasins are based on a rare, pre-Revolutionary War artifact unearthed at the site of Fort Ligonier.

2. Fur caps of various makes, like those made of coonskin, were also worn. In 1766, James Smith returned from a hunting trip with his young servant, the latter in "a bear-skin dressed with the hair on, which he belted about him, and a raccoon-skin cap." Among Pennsylvania ranger George Roush's field attire in the following decade was, in his words, "a cap made out of a raccoon skin, with the feathers of a hawk, painted red, fastened to the top of the cap."

3. Hooded coats made of heavy wool or blanketing were called capotes, cappo coats, blanket coats, or blanket greatcoats. Most often these were white, blue or red in color, with binding sewn along the edges. Many lacked buttons, and were held in place with sash or belt. During Pontiac's War, enraged militiamen of Paxton and Donegal townships, Pennsylvania, marched upon Philadelphia to confront neutral Quaker officials. These rangers were described as "a set of fellows in blanket coats and moccasins, like our Indian traders or back-country wagoners."

4. Contemporary descriptions of the dress of frontiersmen of the 1760s are very rare, but a detachment of 400 Virginia volunteers that went west from Fort Pitt with Colonel Henry Bouquet's army in October 1764 was briefly sketched in a letter to *The Scots Magazine*, and to some degree suggests the field clothing of many Appalachian border rangers of the decade. They were "all armed with rifles, and excellent marksmen, and dressed alamode de sauvages, with painted shirts and fur-caps stained with paint." The "painted" (dyed) shirts may have been forerunners of the ubiquitous fringed hunting shirts of the Revolution. Some of them were probably split in front and wrapped across the chest, as shown in the figure. In his *An Historical Account of Colonel Bouquet's Expedition Against the Ohio Indians in the Year 1764*, William Smith included the papers of an unnamed officer with "long experience … in our wars with the Indians," who suggested that soldiers embarking on such campaigns wear, aside from "an oiled surtout" and other items, "a strong tanned shirt, short trowsers, leggins [and] mokawsons or shoe packs."

5. Another recommendation found in Smith's *Historical Account* is for the soldier "to have a small piece of … oiled linen to put under the hat or cap to carry the rain down to the watchcoat or surtout."

6. Butcher knives, like the wooden-handled one seen here, were worn in belt sheathes and did double duty in both camp and battle.

INDEX

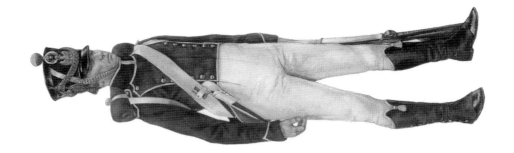 

FIND OUT MORE ABOUT OSPREY

❏ Please send me the latest listing of Osprey's publications

❏ I would like to subscribe to Osprey's e-mail newsletter

Title / rank _____

Name _____

Address _____

_____

City / county _____

Postcode / zip _____ state / country _____

e-mail _____

WAR

I am interested in:

❏ Ancient world
❏ Medieval world
❏ 16th century
❏ 17th century
❏ 18th century
❏ Napoleonic
❏ 19th century

❏ American Civil War
❏ World War 1
❏ World War 2
❏ Modern warfare
❏ Military aviation
❏ Naval warfare

Please send to:

USA & Canada:
Osprey Direct USA, c/o MBI Publishing, P.O. Box 1, 729 Prospect Avenue, Osceola, WI 54020

UK, Europe and rest of world:
Osprey Direct UK, P.O. Box 140, Wellingborough, Northants, NN8 2FA, United Kingdom

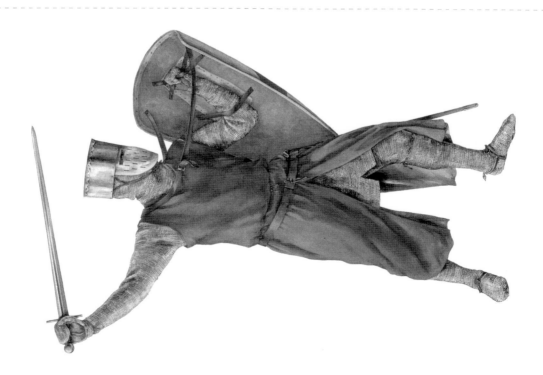

OSPREY
PUBLISHING

www.ospreypublishing.com

call our telephone hotline
for a free information pack

USA & Canada: 1-800-826-6600
UK, Europe and rest of world call:
+44 (0) 1933 443 863

Young Guardsman
Figure taken from *Warrior 22:*
Imperial Guardsman 1799–1815
Published by Osprey
Illustrated by Richard Hook

Knight, c.1190
Figure taken from *Warrior 1: Norman Knight 950 – 1204 AD*
Published by Osprey
Illustrated by Christa Hook

POSTCARD